FIRST OF THE

SPACEMEN

IVEN C. KINCHELOE, Jr.

by James J. Haggerty, Jr.

DUELL, SLOAN AND PEARCE

New York

ACKNOWLEDGMENTS

THE reconstruction of a man's life is a difficult job, a tedious, time-consuming task of collecting and
checking facts. In the case of Iven Kincheloe's exciting and
multi-faceted life, it was particularly difficult, and the research could not have been accomplished without the co-
operation of a great many people. In practically every case,
the author met with complete and enthusiastic co-operation
on the part of Kincheloe's friends and fellow workers. To
these people, the author and publisher are deeply indebted.

First and foremost, there is Kincheloe's devoted widow,
Dorothy, who inspired this book. Dorothy Kincheloe felt
strongly that the world should know more about the exploits
and personality of her late husband. For more than a year
after his death, she pursued the project tirelessly, writing
letters to all his friends and co-workers, now scattered all over
the globe, asking for detailed information about portions of
his career with which she was not familiar. Later, she sub-
mitted to long, trying, memory-provoking hours of inter-
view, helping recapture every detail of Kincheloe's life. She
worked as collaborator and researcher with contagious en-

v

thusiasm. She saw this book as a memorial to the husband she loved, and no task was too great for that cause.

Next, there are Kincheloe's parents, Mr. and Mrs. Iven C. Kincheloe, Sr., who went to considerable pains to recall and recount the early life of their only son, and who made available a very complete file of all the letters he had ever written them.

The author personally interviewed a great many people who had known Kincheloe at one stage or another of his career. It was inspiring to note the vein of unanimity throughout these interviews as regards their laudatory appraisals of the character and flying skill of Iven Kincheloe. Space does not permit listing all these names, but special note must be made of the contributions of the following:

F. W. "Bill" Botts, Jr., who supplied most of the information about Kincheloe's course at the Empire Test Pilots' School; Colonel Francis "Gabby" Gabreski, Kincheloe's Korean commander, and fellow Korean fliers Walker "Bud" Mahurin, William Westcott, Dave Freeland, and Don Rodewald; Bob Hoover, himself an outstanding test pilot, who knew Kincheloe at several stages of his career; General Marcus Cooper, Kincheloe's commander at Edwards Air Force Base; J. Ray Donohue and Siegfried Hanson; and the very cooperative staff of the Air Force Flight Test Center during the author's visit there, most notably Lieutenant Colonels Harold Russel, C. E. Anderson, and Howard M. Lane, Major H. H. Sperber, and civilians Jack Wessesky and Richard Harer.

Then there were the almost one hundred persons who responded by letter to Dorothy Kincheloe's request. Special note must be made of the detailed information provided by Kincheloe's friends in his early flying days, Jim Scheuer, Russ Harmon, Rex Sebastian, and D. D. Overton; Korean fliers Joe Cannon and Major William Whisner; fellow test-pilot

vi

trainees Harry Julian, Tony Blackman, and Major Richard Fernbaugh; and those who knew Kincheloe during his days as a test pilot, Colonel Frank "Pete" Everest, Lou Schalk, Stuart Childs, Bob Lapp, and Jimmy Powell.

Last, but most certainly not least, gratitude must be expressed to two Air Force officers who had great interest in this book and who exerted considerable effort to provide detailed information. They were Major James Sunderman, Chief of the USAF's Book Program, and Colonel Charles A. Brown, Information Officer for the Air Force Flight Test Center.

JAMES J. HAGGERTY, JR.

CONTENTS

ILLUSTRATIONS

following page 84

FIRST OF THE

SPACEMEN

I. INTRODUCTION

IN THE heart of the nation's capital, a block from the White House, is the National Aviation Club, in whose plush premises some two thousand members of the flying fraternity gather for lunch or dinner and exchange hangar talk.

On one wall of the club's popular Men's Bar is a mural, on which artist George Wunder has drawn the faces of eleven men who made outstanding contributions to America's air progress, in war or peace. The faces bear great names, for the most part well known to even the most casual follower of aviation history, so well known, in fact, that their roles in the conquest of the sky need no delineation.

There is Orville Wright, of course; and Billy Mitchell, Charles Lindbergh, Wiley Post, Jimmy Doolittle, Hoyt Vandenberg, Carl Spaatz, Claire Chennault, Eddie Rickenbacker, and H. H. "Hap" Arnold.

The eleventh member of this exclusive company of air greats is Captain Iven C. Kincheloe, Jr., of the United States Air Force. The layman might not immediately recognize this name, for Kincheloe's exposure to the public limelight was brief. To the airman, the name is a famous one, worthy of all the respect due the other faces on the mural.

The name of Kincheloe is memorialized elsewhere. At Purdue University, where he studied aeronautical engineering, a scholarship and a library bear Kincheloe's name, and the Reserve Officers' Training Corps squadron is named in his memory. The top award of the Society of Experimental Test Pilots, to whose glamorous ranks he added luster, is the Iven C. Kincheloe Trophy. The residents of his home town, Cassopolis, Michigan, are erecting a massive twelve-foot stone monument, topped by a three-foot steel model of a rocket airplane, a symbol of their pride in the accomplishments of their native son. In addition, President Eisenhower has personally guaranteed an appointment to the Air Force Academy to Kincheloe's young son Robert when he becomes of age.

One of the highest honors the Air Force can bestow upon one of its heroes is to name an air base in his memory. It is an honor not lightly or often conferred. The Air Force regulation that governs this procedure states that memorializations of this type "must be evaluated with deliberate, unhurried care to insure the selection of only the most deserving individuals." It adds: "Only the names of individuals of *established pre-eminence* will be considered for designating installations. This category includes national heroes and others who have performed duties of great responsibility in an outstanding manner and who have made a major contribution to the development and/or mission of the Air Force."

In naming its bases, the Air Force has scrupulously followed the intent of that regulation. Only the greatest names from the pages of the air service's spectacular history have been selected.

There is Arnold Air Force Base, named for the brilliant and visionary commander of the Army Air Forces, whose

4

successful fight for daytime bombing in the face of opposition speeded the end of World War II. There is Vandenberg Air Force Base, a missile facility bearing the name of the inspired combat leader of World War II who served as Chief of Staff of the Air Force in a later war, the Korean "police action."

There are bases named Andrews, Bolling, Patrick, Ent, and Fairchild. These names and the achievements for which they are honored have become dimmed in man's short memory, but each, in some way, made a substantial contribution to the development of the world's mightiest air force.

The most recent name added to this honor roll of military airmen was that of Captain Iven C. Kincheloe, Jr. With formal dedication ceremonies on September 25, 1959, the home airfield in northern Michigan of the 51st Fighter Group with which he served in the Korean War was named Kincheloe Air Force Base.

Who was this Kincheloe, and what did he do to merit inclusion in the ranks of aviation's elite corps?

Iven Kincheloe was a pilot, but by no means an ordinary one. He lived to fly, and he loved every minute he spent "boring holes in the sky." An aircraft engineer as well as a flier, he knew every detail of construction of every airplane he flew, and he knew how to coax the last iota of performance from the powerful flying machines of his vintage.

He proved it in Korea, where his superb flying skill made him not just an "ace"—by Air Force definition, one who has destroyed five enemy aircraft in combat—but a "double ace," as his blazing guns blasted ten Communist pilots out of the sky.

Korea, though, was just a proving ground for "Kinch." It was after the Korean war that he made his major contributions to the advancement of the art of flight, and to the then embryonic field of space research.

As an experimental test pilot for the Air Force, Kincheloe flew just about every type of military airplane built during the middle and late fifties, a period of explosive technological progress that brought forth planes capable of flying at two and three times the speed of sound.

It was in a little, rock-ribbed, rocket-powered manned-missile called the X-2 that he flew his most spectacular missions. On one such flight, more than two years before a Soviet satellite penetrated the earth's rind of atmosphere and officially started the Space Age, Kincheloe and the X-2 rocketed to the incredible height of 126,200 feet. Almost twenty-four miles above the surface, at an altitude from which he could see hundreds of miles in any direction and make out the earth's contour, he witnessed the blinding glory of the sun, undistorted by the dense layers of atmospheric molecules which dim its radiance to the view of earth-bound man. With more than 99½ per cent of the atmosphere beneath the stubby wings of his vehicle, Kincheloe was in space, according to one definition of where space begins by the National Aeronautics and Space Administration. His work on the X-2 program earned Kincheloe two of the nation's top aviation awards, the Air Force's McKay Trophy and the Air Force Association's David C. Schilling Memorial Trophy.

Kincheloe's continuing researches into space lore, both in the air and in a series of laboratory tests on the ground, qualified him as one of America's space pioneers. Although a very junior officer, he was sought out by the highest-ranking generals, who frequently asked his advice on projects under consideration, as did top scientists and other space researchers.

Kinch was, to use his own term, a "space bug." He knew, before a *sputnik* spread wide the belief, that man would penetrate farther into space, and when that came about, he was determined that he would be one of the penetrators.

6

A novelist drawing a "superman" character might well have used Kincheloe as his model. He was tall and handsome, powerfully built, mentally brilliant, highly articulate, always calm in emergencies, yet he was warm and human, possessed of a lively sense of humor, full of youthful enthusiasms. His life was exciting and colorful, a tale of high adventure, and some of its chapters would tax the novelist's imagination.

The life of Iven Kincheloe is more than an account of one man's existence, his hopes and fear, his joys and sorrows, his daring feats. It is a story about that rare breed of mankind, test pilots, who live under the motto *"Ad Inexplorata"*— Toward the Unknown—men of vision and skill and courage who thrill to the adventure of probing new realms of the mysterious world that stretches upward from the earth's surface and outward to infinity. They are men who know well the risks of their hazardous profession, but who would have no other. They rejoice in the feeling that they are stars in the daily drama of life, not just spectators of the passing scene, for with each flight they are adding a little more to man's accumulated knowledge of the universe.

Iven Kincheloe was one of the outstanding members of this great and colorful fraternity. This is his story.

II. THE START OF THE DREAM

IN THE latter nineteen twenties, aviation was growing up rapidly, its practicability as a mode of transport becoming more and more apparent due to a number of spectacular pioneering flights.

In 1927, a lanky, towheaded youngster named Charles Lindbergh took off from New York in a little, single-engine monoplane and flew it more than 3,600 miles nonstop to Paris, a great feat which stirred the imagination of the world and brought new faith in that odd contraption, the airplane.

A little more than a month later, a pair of Army lieutenants named Maitland and Hegenberger made the first nonstop flight from Oakland to Honolulu.

In 1928, the twenty-fifth anniversary of powered flight, new air-transport companies were inaugurating scheduled passenger service all over the United States and the series of record flights continued. In April of that year, Captain Sir George Hubert Wilkins and Lieutenant Carl Eielson made a sensational 2,200-mile flight over the "top of the world," from Point Barrow, Alaska, to Green Harbor, Spitsbergen. In May, an Army lieutenant named Royal Thomas set a new endurance record, topping even Lindbergh's time in the air, with a thirty-five-hour twenty-five-minute flight in a single-engine airplane. In June, Amelia Earhart became the first woman pilot to cross the Atlantic.

On July 2, a baby son who was one day to share a mural of aviation greats with Lindbergh was born in Detroit to Iven and Frances Kincheloe. His parents named him Iven, Jr.

Young Iven's interest in airplanes started as early as a child can become interested in anything. He was three years old when his parents moved to a farm in Cassopolis, Michigan. Iven, Sr., had been in the engineering department of Graham-Paige Motors in Detroit until the Great Depression struck the automobile industry and thousands were dropped from the payrolls.

The Kincheloes were more fortunate than millions of luckless others who suffered through those lean years. The farm in Cassopolis had been in the family for generations. It was not a big farm, but it offered a living. Iven, Sr., became a farmer.

One Sunday he took his wife and son to a nearby airfield at Grosse Ile to watch the airplanes. Lindbergh and his fellow airmen of that day had aroused great interest in flying machines. Few were so intrepid as to take a ride in one, but plane-watching had become a big Sunday-afternoon spectator sport.

The planes of that day were not much by today's standards. They were little flimsy crates of cloth and plywood, with open cockpits and engines that sputtered and biplane wings held together by struts and baling wire. But to young Iven Kincheloe they were magnificent vehicles that could fly higher and faster than the birds. It was the start of a dream.

Sunday plane-watching became standard practice for the Kincheloes, at the youngster's insistence. He would watch in awe and fascination as the little Wacos and Stearmans and Stinsons chugged into the air, and his rapturous gaze would follow them far into the sky until they droned out of sight.

In April of 1933 came a big moment in the young life of Iven Kincheloe. On the Kincheloe farm was a small landing strip, built years earlier by the Government as an emergency field for its airmail pilots. One day, a barnstorming pilot dropped around to see the senior Kincheloe, to ask permission to use the field for a flight exhibition that would include selling two-dollar rides to the locals.

Kincheloe, Sr., as interested in airplanes as anybody, agreed readily and waived his rental fee in exchange for a plane ride for young Iven.

It was a never-to-be-forgotten experience. Iven's baby face was a study in ecstasy as the biplane lifted off the ground. His waving parents grew smaller and smaller and the familiar farmland took on a new magic as he viewed it from above. When he was lifted out of the cockpit half an hour later, he was speechless with the thrill of this great experience.

From that day on, airplanes were uppermost in Iven's thoughts. He had other boyish interests, of course. He loved to do simple chores about the farm, like milking the cows and feeding the chickens. He spent a lot of time with his pets. There were the two cats, Peter and Pan, and the big dog, Chief, who was half police dog and half collie. And there was Worser, a white pig that Iven acquired when it was small enough to live in a little home he made for it out of a gallon can. Iven had a collar and leash for Worser, and it amused the residents of Cassopolis to see the blond, blue-eyed youngster leading the pig, who had rapidly outgrown his gallon-size home, on their daily walks.

But even Worser, who was the favorite pet, took second place in Iven's youthful interest to airplanes—watching them,

10

flying in them, and building them. When he was not quite five, he started building model planes. His parents encouraged the hobby and provided him with all the materials he needed, with one stipulation: he must finish every one he started, an edict which probably founded the determined, stick-to-it-iveness which characterized his later life. At an age when most children found it difficult to make a symmetrical mud pie, Iven developed a high degree of skill in assembling aircraft, a skill which stemmed from his intense interest in the details of each component of the model plane.

In the fall of his fifth year, he started school at the Penn School in Penn Township, about a mile from Kincheloe farm. It was one of those clapboard rural schools with only one teacher and sometimes only one pupil in a grade, although most grades had four or five.

Iven loved to learn, and he tackled education with charac-teristic intensity, displaying as early as kindergarten the in-satiable thirst for knowledge that was to drive him into all sorts of advanced aeronautical research in later years. The routine subjects of the grammar grades came easily to him, and he would frequently undertake study projects beyond those assigned him, as though he were already conscious of the little time he had to learn everything there was to know.

His early individuality of thought was pointed up during the preparations for the annual Penn School Christmas play when Iven was a fifth-grade student. Teacher Elsie McFee, possibly influenced by the interests of her prize student, had changed the traditional Christmas script. Santa Claus was to leave his famed reindeer at home and make his rounds by airplane. Practically everyone in the school wanted the star part, that of Santa. Not Iven Kincheloe; he wanted to be Santa's pilot, because obviously flying the airplane took a great deal more skill than slipping down chimneys with a bag of toys. He got the part.

Because he skipped a grade in grammar school, Iven, or Carl, as he was now known, was just past thirteen when he entered Dowagiac High School, although he tried to "let on" he was older. In physical appearance he did not look even thirteen; he was slightly built, not very tall, his features good-looking but still babyish. Yet his adult manner of thinking and speaking made him seem older, and he was usually accepted as the leader in any student enterprise.

From the start of his high-school days, Iven had his career mapped out. His youthful enthusiasm for airplanes and flying had never waned; it had, in fact, become more intense. He decided he wanted to be an aeronautical engineer, and although his parents thought a career in law or medicine might be more attractive, they never sought to discourage him. The Kincheloes were always very close to their only son, and if he thought the air was his niche in life, that's what it would be.

With typical Kincheloe drive, he went to work on his career-planning. Ironically, the one subject in which he was not completely proficient was mathematics, the one most important to an engineer. Iven tackled it grimly, staying after school, studying at nights, assigning himself homework beyond the school requirements. He never quite met his own standards of math perfection, but he had set the standards so high that even falling short of them made him an outstanding math student.

He read and he read and he read, until he almost exhausted the stock of aviation literature. He built up his own small library, ranging from juvenile air fiction like *The Daredevils of the Air* and *The Airship Boys* to highly technical trade magazines. He haunted the Dowagiac public library until he

12

had read every aviation book on its shelves, then pestered the librarian to find new ones. Impressed by the youngster's ambitious reading program, the librarian entered into the spirit of the game and took delight in coming up with volumes of which even young Kincheloe had not known. He read all of them.

Yet Iven was not a complete bookworm. Somehow he found time for a wide range of activities. He took up drums, and learned to play them well enough to sit in the school orchestra. He doubled as student manager of the high-school band. He was active in the 4-H Club and the Sea Scouts. He worked on the school paper and participated in the student council, becoming president in his senior year. He was a top-ranking member of the Dowagiac High School track team, and although he was still too small to play on the varsity football and basketball teams, he went out for the "B" squads and played each game as though it were the Rose Bowl. He fished and hunted, and became an expert marksman. In everything he tried, he sought perfection—and usually came close to it.

In the summer of 1942, with his fourteenth birthday just behind him, Iven convinced his parents that he was old enough to learn to fly. He was already driving a car, an antiquated prewar Chevy he was allowed to operate under a special Michigan law because he had to commute fourteen miles each way to and from school. He argued that if he could drive a car, he could fly a plane. Kincheloe, Sr., on whom some of Iven's flying enthusiasm had rubbed off, felt he would like to try it himself.

Together father and son went to nearby Niles Airport and enrolled for a course of instruction under Leland Roskay, the airport manager. The elder Kincheloe became a competent pilot, but Roskay had never seen anything like the younger

Kincheloe. Mentally Iven had already been flying for ten years, since his first short hop around the farm. Repeated "two-dollar rides" over the years had made him completely at home in the air and his years of reading had taught him a great deal about handling the controls. After only two flying hours of instruction, Lee Roskay shook his head.

"I don't believe it," he confided to Kincheloe, Sr. "I could send him off solo right now, but I can't do it officially. The law says he has to be sixteen."

So for two impatient years, Iven sweated out his first solo. He worked on perfecting his climbing turns and his diving turns, his stalls and spins, and long before he was able to solo officially he was doing advanced aerobatics. He was even making difficult pontoon landings in the snow on the farm. Roskay, recognizing in Iven a flying prodigy, taught him everything he knew, until the skill gap between instructor and student became a very narrow one. To comply with the law, Roskay (or another instructor after Roskay took a wartime job as a test pilot with an aircraft company) went along with Iven on every flight, but it was usually just for the ride.

On July 2, 1944, his sixteenth birthday, Iven Kincheloe soloed "for the record." With a couple of hundred hours of flying experience behind him and his thorough knowledge of everything connected with flying, from airplane design and structure to the physical laws of flight, with his innate flying skill and his superior co-ordination, Iven Kincheloe was probably the most proficient pilot ever to solo in the state of Michigan, maybe anywhere.

And yet, to Iven, the solo was anything but routine. There is something about going aloft alone for the first time that brings a new thrill to flying. You are alone with the magnificence of nature and you have a godlike feeling of power as you conquer her gravity. You are Man at his finest as your brain and muscular skill direct the flying machine through the sky. To sixteen-year-old Iven Kincheloe, who had lived most of his young life toward this moment, it was a sublime experience. If there had ever been the slightest doubt about the course of his future, it disappeared in the air over Niles Airport on that great day.

For the next year, his last in high school, Iven lived to fly. He saved his allowance and took on odd jobs like pumping gas to make extra money, and practically all of it went into flying time. As soon as he obtained his license, he took his mother up as his first passenger. Later, he flew some of his schoolmates.

Naturally, he was a Hero Grade One at Dowagiac High School; although, in the war years, airplanes were no longer novelties, a teen-age pilot was really something. To his school-girl friends, good-looking, personable, witty Iven Kincheloe took on a new glamour, but Iven had little time for girls. There were too many things to do.

As graduation approached, Iven prepared in his methodical way for college. The Kincheloes had never become wealthy, but the farm had brought them a comfortable living and there was enough money for college. As early as his sophomore year in high school, Iven had started his characteristically thorough research on universities. He sent all over the country for catalogues and studied curriculums carefully; he talked with his flying instructors and others in aviation, to his teachers and anyone he felt might know something about the subject, building a volume of comparative data on colleges. Which one had the best football team, which offered the most attractive campus life, all the other pros and cons his classmates debated carried no weight with Iven. Which offered him the best grounding for a career in aviation? That was the measure by which they were judged.

15

He considered and researched the possibilities of the Naval, Military, and Coast Guard Academies, but found that he was too young. He would have to wait a year after graduation from high school and the thought was unbearable.

In his senior year, he made his decision. Weighing the subordinate factors, like tuition and distance from home, with the important things, like curricular excellence and the availability of an Air Reserve Officers' Training Corps program, Iven settled on Purdue University at Lafayette, Indiana. As nearly as he could determine, Purdue's school of aeronautical engineering had no peer, and the University had an Air R.O.T.C. squadron which would help prepare him for advanced flight training. So Purdue it was.

Graduation came and Iven whiled away the summer, flying whenever he could, doing chores around the farm, and boning up on math, in which he was now very competent, but Iven was not one to fluff a great opportunity for lack of a little advance headwork. World War II came to a sudden end with the twin nuclear mushrooms of Hiroshima and Nagasaki, erasing Iven's half-formed dream of becoming a great combat flyer as a prelude to his engineering career. Then it was fall, and he was off to Lafayette, impatient to start the new phase of his life as an airman.

III. COLLEGE DAYS

At PURDUE, Iven, or Carl, as he was usually called there, found he was even more of a "baby" than he had been in high school. Where he had usually been a year younger than his classmates, the gap had widened. Purdue was jammed with eager young veterans of World War II, taking advantage of the opportunity to get a free education from the Government under the "GI Bill." Their ages ranged from the early to the late twenties; Iven was barely seventeen.

He looked even younger. He had grown taller, a little under six feet, but he was slightly built. His thin but good-looking face was still babyish, and the shock of white-blond hair that romped over his forehead in unruly disarray added to the boyish look. Only the penetrating blue eyes, which made some of his classmates feel as though he were looking right through them and reading their thoughts, gave him an appearance of maturity. He had big "Clark Gable" ears, and his friends, using a phrase of that day, said he looked like a yellow cab coming down the street with its back doors open.

Despite the difference in ages, Iven was immediately accepted as "one of the boys." There was something about him that made you forget his youthful appearance—perhaps the thoughtful, deliberate manner in which he conversed, or the way he listened to what you had to say, intently, as though you were making a major pronunciamento when you might only be suggesting a stroll to the drugstore for a Coke.

Iven was a born "brain-picker," and the Purdue campus provided him with a wealth of material. Among the horde of World War II veterans, there were a great many "flyboys"—pilots, navigators, bombardiers, gunners, mechanics. Iven sought them out and picked their brains casually, never seeming to ask too many questions, but encouraging them to talk about planes and combat techniques. He learned a great deal from them, and they occasionally learned something from him, for the hastily trained men of the Army Air Forces knew surprisingly little about their aircraft. Iven could contribute to the conversation by telling them intricate details of the construction of the B-17 or the involved workings of its power plants, things they had never learned in the helter-skelter, "quick-and-dirty" war-training programs.

So despite his age and despite their experience, Iven became the acknowledged aviation expert of his group; this occasionally caused him embarrassment, when someone who did not know him well would ask, "What outfit were you with?" Iven, always reluctant to admit he had been too young for the war, although it was well known to his closer friends, would mumble something about having "stayed stateside during the war."

He was pledged to the Sigma Phi Epsilon fraternity and he plunged into a round of extracurricular activity. Still too small for the varsity, he played center on intramural football squads and the "B" team. In his freshman year, he became track manager and held the post throughout his four years at Purdue. He was a member of several major dance committees, and, as he had planned to, he became very active in the Air Reserve Officers' Training Corps squadron at Purdue.

The Air R.O.T.C. was not a flying operation. Instead, it trained future reserve officers in ground subjects, ranging from the wearing of the uniform and the proper method of saluting to advanced air-combat techniques, offering them commissions as second lieutenants in the Army Air Force upon graduation.

With his typical intensity, Iven worked hard on the R.O.T.C. end of his college career. He became a member of the Scabbard and Blade military honorary society and he made cadet officer in the R.O.T.C. He took a lot of ribbing about that. The baby-faced youngster in his fancy uniform, complete with sword, made a ludicrous picture to the combat veterans of World War II, and they let him have it.

Iven took the ribbing good-naturedly. With his crooked grin, he would say:

"Laugh, you hyenas, but you're in trouble when I make general."

For all his extracurricular activity, Iven was a good student. For the most part, the work came easily. Math, which had bothered him, turned out to be no problem at all, and most of the other subjects he could handle without too much "boning." Only one—applied mechanics—gave him real trouble, and he tackled that in characteristic Kincheloe fashion: get help from the people who know. He sought out a frat brother, Earl Van Horne, who was a "hot man" on applied mechanics, and confessed his inability to master the subject. Van Horne, one of the war vets, took an immediate liking to the "kid" and devoted long hours of his own time to explaining the involved subject. He quickly got to the root of Iven's trouble—he was memorizing formulas instead of trying to figure out what they meant—and while Iven never became a star student in applied mechanics, he had considerably less trouble with the course thereafter.

The engineering course was a real challenge to Iven; it was a fascinating polish to the years he had spent studying airplanes since the time he had started making models. A number of his classmates were not so enthusiastic about aeronautical engineering. In the year following the end of World War II, a drastic reduction in aircraft manufacture had taken place. The companies which had turned out fighters and bombers by the tens of thousands were now building only a few planes a month, and they were laying off personnel, including engineers, in great numbers. Aero engineering no longer seemed the opportunity-laden career it had been thought to be during the war years.

Iven Kincheloe did not share this view. It was more of a career than ever, he argued. Sure, they were dropping engineers by the ton, but there was an even greater need for *good* engineers.

The jet engine had come along during the war, and jet aircraft like the P-80 were just beginning to appear in numbers. They could cruise about the sky at an unheard-of 550 miles per hour, but to visionary Iven Kincheloe this was nothing. He recognized the inherent potential of this new type of power, and he argued that planes would soon be flying faster than sound, a subject of considerable debate among students and even among engineers in those early postwar years.

Supersonic flight, he felt, would put a new tax upon the ingenuity of aircraft designers and he dove into his textbooks with vigor, determined to be the best aeronautical engineer in the business.

It was fascinating work. He learned more and more about the eternal compromise of aircraft design, the need for so

20

much power to drive so much weight at a given speed, the requirement for building components stronger, to resist the impact of speed, yet lighter, so the speed could be attained. This, he decided, was his real niche in life.

And while he pursued his engineering studies, he never lost the urge to fly. Designing planes was one thing, a thrill of a special kind, but nothing could ever replace the magic feeling of "boring holes in the sky."

With no airplane to fly at Purdue, Iven set about finding one. With Wally Bolt, veteran, he formed a flying club composed of a dozen amateur pilots. They pooled their money and bought a surplus PT-19, a two-seat open-cockpit trainer the Army had used during the war. Theoretically they flew in turn, but somehow Iven Kincheloe's turn seemed to come up more often.

It was in April, 1946, that Iven experienced his first aircraft accident. He talked Wally Bolt into taking the PT-19 on a cross-country visit to the Kincheloe farm in Cassopolis. As they came in for a landing on the old strip where Iven had first gone aloft as a child, Iven, at the controls, overlooked an R.E.A. power line. He dove under it at the last split second, but the wire clipped his right wing tip, then ripped through the top of the rudder. He wobbled in to a near-stall landing.

Their visit with the senior Kincheloes concluded, the two student engineers surveyed their torn plane. Applying their tyro knowledge of aerodynamics, and weighing in a strong luck factor, they decided they could make it back to Purdue, and somehow managed it.

The ribbing was unmerciful in the frat house. Whenever Iven joined a group, they would start on him.

"Hot pilot, indeed!"

"On his own farm, yet!"

And Iven would grin his crooked grin and say:

"I'm a test pilot for R.E.A. I was testing the strength of that wire."

During Memorial Day vacation in his sophomore year, Iven acquired a new love, one which had a lot in common with airplanes, the thrill of skill applied to power: racing automobiles. He did not get to race any cars, but he learned a lot about them in a brief job at famed Indianapolis Speedway, where the nation's top auto races are run annually on Memorial Day.

Iven was given the resounding title of Deputy Marshal for Special Services, and permitted to wear a white helmet. The special services, for the most part, included running errands, but Iven didn't mind. He met all the great race drivers, learned about their cars and engines, and decided that here was something else he must do someday—drive a racing auto. It was not to be a part of his career, of course, but a hobby, to be taken up when he became a wealthy design engineer. He went back to the track as Deputy Marshal each year throughout his college days.

Iven's ready wit and readiness for a prank, his ever-cheerful, friendly manner, and his wide range of extracurricular activities brought him a great many friends at Purdue. Two of the closest were Jim Scheuer and Victor "Bud" Kupferer, both of whom, like Iven, had dreamed of becoming pilots since they were "knee-high to crabgrass," as Scheuer put it.

It was in the summer of 1947 that Iven Kincheloe's career aspirations took on a slightly different aspect—not really a change in direction, just a slight bend. It was a hot, sticky morning at Purdue University Airport, where the engineering school had a few old airplanes for ground-test demonstrations.

Iven and Scheuer watched for a while as a wingless wartime

P-47 whirled about a pivot on a concrete slab, its engine roaring and its propeller spinning rapidly. The odd-looking rig had a purpose: the propeller was instrumented with strain gauges to determine the stress on the prop while the old fuselage spun wildly.

Then they made their way up into the cockpit of another old war klunker, a C-46 transport, and sat in the pilots' seats watching the stress test, the muffled roar of the P-47's engine drifting over to them.

Iven turned to Scheuer.

"You know, Jim, that's for me."

"What?" asked Scheuer, looking toward the test rig. "Propellers?"

"No, no, no. You know what I mean. Test flying. Engineering is great, but just look at the fun we could have if we could fly and check our own data."

Scheuer looked doubtful.

"Well—"

"Look at the experience these vets in our class have had," Iven continued earnestly. "Aircraft companies aren't going to take us before they take them. We're too young. So why don't we go through advanced flight training and *then* look for a job in the industry?"

It was a new idea and it started both of them thinking. It made sense. Iven was still confident that he would be a better engineer than his classmates, but how do you get a chance to prove it? The aeronautical-engineering profession was still getting tighter and jobs would be scarce on graduation.

On the other hand, suppose they could get an Air Force commission and spend a few years getting experience and very advanced training in some of the new jets coming along. Then they could go to a company doubly armed, because engineering test pilots were hard to come by. The test-pilot profession had acquired maturity during the war; its members no longer wore white scarves carelessly flung over the shoulder, the way the movies depicted them. They didn't plunge an airplane into a vertical dive until the wings came off, then bail out to report the flaw in the design.

The postwar test pilot was dealing with advanced, high-speed aircraft of ever-increasing complexity. In testing it, he had to be thoroughly familiar with its every component. The designers did not want a pilot to come down from a test flight and report that wing flutter had developed at Mach .82. They wanted someone who could not only note the phenomenon, but advance an opinion as to *why* it had developed. Thus, the prime requirement for test pilots had become an engineering degree, and limited indeed was the number of men who had the skill and courage to be test pilots and the intelligence and vision required of aeronautical engineers.

Iven and Scheuer and the third member of their trio, Kupferer, mulled over this new idea through their junior year at Purdue, and the following summer, 1948, their minds were made up; at least, Iven's was made up, and he prevailed upon the others.

It was the R.O.T.C. summer encampment that did it. This, a six-week course at Wright-Patterson Air Force Base at Dayton, Ohio, was the young cadets' first real taste of Air Force life. It consisted of courses of instruction at the various laboratories at Wright-Pat, inspection of all the latest models of aircraft undergoing test at the base, and the usual monotonous but necessary drill and field-camping.

Iven went to brain-picking in earnest among the officers of the base, and those whose brains he picked most thoroughly were two great test pilots—Bob Hoover and Charles "Chuck" Yeager. Yeager, then a captain, had only a few months earlier become the first man to fly faster than sound, dispelling forever the myth of a "sound barrier" which would cause planes to disintegrate as their speed matched that of sound.

Yeager, already a celebrity because of his great experience, was weary of the barrage of questions he received whenever he met a new acquaintance, but with this blond young R.O.T.C. cadet it was different. The questions were sharper and they indicated far more than surface knowledge of the problems of supersonic flight. Impressed by the eagerness of young Kincheloe, the sincere and unquenchable thirst for more knowledge, Yeager gave him a detailed "fill-in" on his memorable flight.

The plane in which Yeager had flown faster than sound was also at Wright-Pat. It was a little, stub-winged plane of Gibraltar-like construction, powered by a mighty rocket engine. Called the X-1, it had been built by Bell Aircraft Corporation of Buffalo, New York. Its potential top speed was about 1,500 miles per hour, in those days more than twice as fast as the latest operational Air Force jet, but Yeager had taken it only to the vicinity of 1,000 miles an hour.

That was good enough for Iven Kincheloe. To him, Yeager was an idol and the little X-1 a shrine. He was permitted to sit in the tiny cockpit and finger the controls, and he dreamed of the day when he would sit in this plane, or one like it, and blast through the sky at incredible speeds, exploring new frontiers of speed and altitude.

His chance meeting with Yeager, who was later to become a close friend, had decided Iven's future once and for all. He would go into the Air Force, become a test pilot, and later, when age dulled his reflexes, he would turn to designing planes.

During the R.O.T.C. summer encampment, he also managed to scrounge a ride in one of the newer Air Force planes, a big bomber called the Boeing B-50. It was not a jet, but it had plenty of "get-up-and-go." To his parents Iven wrote a long letter, detailing every step of this momentous flight, adding, "I think I have found what I *really* want to do now."

Back at Purdue, he talked it over with Scheuer and Kupferer, his air-minded buddies. They agreed that flight training in the military service seemed to be the thing to try, but Scheuer, to Iven's intense disgust, had come up with a new wrinkle—he wanted to go into naval aviation. Iven, already a loyal Air Force man, would have none of that, and they argued about it all year.

In his senior year, Iven intensified his already intense study program, because now he had a real goal and he was not going to let academic standing become an obstacle to his getting an Air Force commission. The days of mass recruiting were over, and the U.S.A.F. could afford to pick and choose among the large number of R.O.T.C. cadets graduating each year.

Nonetheless, he also stepped up his extracurricular activity. He became an active participant in the Societies of Aeronautical, Mechanical, and Automotive Engineering, the Spiked Shoe Club, and the Skymotive Club. He got a job on *The Exponent*, the campus newspaper. He was elected to the P-Men's Club, helped plan the Military Ball, and was chairman of the Purdue Relays committee, an annual track-and-field event. His greatest collegiate honor came with his election to the highly respected honorary Gimlet Club as an outstanding fraternity man who boosted Purdue athletics and traditions.

His flying ability came in handy in the fall of 1948, on the eve of the traditional "Old Oaken Bucket" football game. In the pregame high jinks between the students of Indiana University and Purdue, a group of I.U. students raided the Purdue campus, let all the air out of every auto tire they could find, and littered the university grounds with pamphlets telling of Purdue's absolute inability to muster a football team worthy of winning the "Bucket."

The student council called Iven and his PT-19 into action. Hastily they printed a counter-leaflet predicting slaughter of the inept Indiana squad. Iven flew to the Indiana campus, did a startlingly low buzz job over the grounds, and when he had attracted sufficient attention, let go ten thousand leaflets. It was acclaimed as a masterful job of morale destruction.

Shortly after the first of the year, in 1949, Iven and Bud Kupferer scored a major point on Jim Scheuer. They convinced him that naval aviation was a thing of the past and that the real future lay in the Air Force. They made a tripartite agreement to apply for flight training.

Through the Air R.O.T.C., they filed their applications and took their physical examinations. Iven and Scheuer passed with flying colors, but Kupferer's clearance was held up pending study of his X rays. Kupferer was O.K.'d by the medics later, but the delay was to place him one class behind his two friends.

Passing the physical, however, did not mean that one was automatically "in." For a couple of months, they "sweated out" the decision of the Air Force selection board, then, in the spring, came the great news: upon completion of their Purdue courses, they would be accepted for flight training.

The last two months of college days dragged by, and then graduation was upon them. Iven did not finish at the top of his class, but he was high enough up the ladder to satisfy even his meticulous requirements. In June, he received a degree of Bachelor of Science in Aeronautical Engineering. Simultaneously, through the Air R.O.T.C, he was commissioned a second lieutenant in the United States Air Force Reserve and assigned to active duty as a student officer flight trainee at Perrin Air Force Base, Texas.

Iven took a brief vacation to visit his parents at Cassopolis; then, in the new Pontiac they had given him as a graduation present, he took off for Sherman, Texas, the home of Perrin Air Force Base, to start still another phase of his aviation career.

IV. KINCH GETS HIS AIR FORCE WINGS

It was on July 9, 1949, that Iven Kincheloe drove through the gates of Perrin Air Force Base. He was no longer a baby-faced youth. In his last year at Purdue, he had attained his full growth. He now stood an inch and a half over six feet tall and weighed in at about 185. His shoulders had broadened, and he had developed a powerful chest and arms. The blond hair was as unruly as ever, and his ears still "flapped in the breeze," but Iven had become a handsome specimen of manhood. With budding maturity, his sense of humor had sharpened, his quick wit had become quicker.

He hunted up Jim Scheuer, who was already on the field, and together they inspected their new base, feeling as conspicuous as only shiny new second lieutenants can feel, all the more so because they were among the first student officers to enter training at Perrin.

Scheuer, he found, was going to be married, and Iven was to be best man. Iven had thought about marriage now and then, but never long enough to pursue it actively. There had been a couple of girls during his Purdue days, one of them an "almost-serious thing," but Iven had decided that marriage was something that could wait. In a letter to his parents, he wrote:

"There are three things an Air Force officer can't use:

1. The sky above him
2. The runway behind him
3. A wife."

It was at Perrin that Iven Carl Kincheloe, Jr., variously known throughout his first twenty-one years as Junior, Iven, and Carl, became once and for all Kinch. Someone tagged him with it and it stuck.

And it was at Perrin that he picked up another very close friend, a South Carolinian with the impressive name of Dolphin D. Overton III, who quickly became "D. D." D. D. was to play an important part in Kinch's later life.

Kinch had had no qualms about flight training. With hundreds of flying hours behind him, he felt it would be a breeze. He got a rude shock. The first thing he was told to do was to "forget" all his previous flying experience. The Air Force was not training commercial pilots but combat fighters, and it had its own carefully programed methods of teaching based on years of experience with young fledglings. Prior training was more frequently a handicap than an asset, because a young pilot improperly trained was liable to pick up some bad habits of which he could not rid himself.

Kinch was a member of Class 50-D, composed mostly of cadets, with a few student officers like himself. For once he was not the "kid" of the class; he was older than most of the cadets and his shiny gold bars gave him added stature. As usual, Kinch quickly became the class leader.

The routine consisted of ground classes in the morning on navigation, meteorology, theory of flight, power plants, and allied subjects, and flying training in the afternoon. The ground school was a "pushover," as he wrote his parents; most of the subjects he had been studying since he was ten.

Flying was something else again. Always one to recognize good advice, Kinch had "forgotten" all he knew about flying. The trainer, though, was a big one—a T-6 Texan, with a big 550-horsepower engine, far bigger than anything he had ever flown. It was the perfect training airplane, but it demanded a high degree of skill, and that was the way the Air Force wanted it. The training officers didn't want anyone to "squeak by," because the next phase would bring even trickier airplanes, which could kill the inept pilot.

His instructor was a captain, Erwin R. Silsbee. Kinch took to Silsbee immediately and the instructor recognized in Kinch one of those "born pilots" it is a real pleasure to instruct.

Perrin was only the first half of the training program. There Class 50-D would get one hundred hours of training in the T-6, and there, too, half of the class would be "washed out." The survivors would go on to one of three types of advanced training, depending upon the aptitudes they displayed in basic school. There was multi-engine advanced, single-engine advanced—conventional (which meant propeller-driven aircraft), and the one everyone wanted but few would get, single-engine jet. There was no question as to which Kinch wanted—it *had* to be jet.

Although he carefully "forgot" his prior training, he could not "forget" his natural skill in an airplane, and Kinch quickly became the "hot pilot" of 50-D. On September 2, 1949, another of those milestone days in the life of Iven Kincheloe, he became the first member of 50-D and the first student officer ever to solo at Perrin. He was accorded the traditional ceremonial rite of being thrown under a shower fully clothed.

And shortly thereafter, to his intense embarrassment, he had the second of his series of aircraft accidents—a ground loop which wrinkled a wing tip and left Kinch unharmed except for severe damage to his ego.

The course progressed swiftly, through basic maneuvers to acrobatics and formation flight, then to instrument flight, a transition which lost a good part of the class but which Kinch relished because it was something new he had not yet tried in an airplane.

As 50-D, its numbers depleted, neared the end of the basic course, the "sweat" was on as to who would get the coveted assignments to jets. There was no question about Kinch, for if ever there was a jet-pilot prospect in the Air Force, it was Iven Kincheloe. So Kinch helped Scheuer and Overton "sweat it out." They both made it.

They graduated from basic school in March, 1950, and moved on to Williams Air Force Base in Arizona, home of the Jet Fighter School.

Kinch took to the jet like a duck to water. Gone was the familiar old propeller, with its speed limitations, its vibrations, and its torque. The jet engine permitted *real* flight. The TF-80 trainer handled like a dream and enhanced all of Kinch's flying skills.

One incident marred Kinch's jet-training course. On one of his early flights in the TF-80, he was flying at 30,000 feet, the highest he had ever been, when his cockpit canopy blew off. The pressurized air in the cockpit escaped in a blast which the Air Force medics call "explosive decompression" and left him exposed to the thin, rarefied upper atmosphere. He became giddy and started to black out, but he had enough presence of mind to put the plane in a steep dive.

Kinch managed to retain consciousness and keep control of the TF-80 until he pulled out at 6,000 feet. He felt weak and dizzy and his head was pounding, but he was able to guide the plane back to Williams for a landing.

The experience left him ill for several days. "It kind of raised hell with the blood vessels in my head," he wrote home, "and apparently caused some damage to the sinuses. I have had terrific headaches since."

Despite the headaches, Kinch was taking no chances with the Air Force medics. The wash-out rate was high at Williams, and he felt something like this might have a serious effect on his own chances of completing the course. So, hiding his ailment from the medics, he went to Phoenix to a civilian doctor for treatment. The headaches cleared up in a few days.

Again Kinch was the hot pilot of the class as 50-D slipped rapidly through advanced training. The training took on new purpose in June, 1950, when war broke out in Korea and the United States Air Force, its forces sadly depleted in the economy wave that had preceded Korea, started to muster its limited squadrons for action in the Orient.

The war came as a shock to most members of 50-D. They had been training for a leisurely life in the peacetime regular Air Force. Now came the sudden realization that they were the prime candidates for the firing line. The Air Force could not recall its World War II vets; few of them had ever sat in a jet cockpit. Those already in operational line groups would be the first sent to Korea; right behind them would come the new trainees, because there just were not enough forces to meet the demands of a war. There would be a brief period of operational training, of course, but within a year after graduation from "Willy Air Patch," the members of 50-D could count on being in combat.

Even a war on the horizon could not dim Kinch's enthusiasm for a flying career. In mid-July, as 50-D was being put through its final training rounds prior to graduation, he wrote his parents that he would probably soon be in Korea and that he was looking forward to it. Combat flying was a real test of a pilot's ability, he said, and furthermore, it offered a chance of more rapid promotion.

Graduation came on August 4, 1950. The senior Kincheloes drove down to Williams A.F.B. from Michigan to attend the celebration, complete with a dress parade and a formation fly-by. Kinch's mother, almost as proud as her big, blond son, pinned on the silver wings which certified that Iven Kincheloe was now a full-fledged Air Force pilot.

Kinch had drawn a coveted assignment to Selfridge Air Force Base, an Air Defense Command jet installation not too far from his home in Cassopolis. His outfit, while preparing for Korea, was to be the top-drawer 56th Fighter Group, commanded by Colonel Francis "Gabby" Gabreski, a World War II ace and one of the great fighter pilots of all time.

Kinch said his good-bys to Scheuer and Overton, who were being assigned elsewhere, and drove back with his parents to Cassopolis for a brief vacation before reporting to Selfridge. He had never been more eager to "get on with the job." All the years of study and training were about to bear fruit. Impatiently he fretted through his vacation, fearful lest the 56th Fighter Group depart for Korea before he joined them.

V. PREPARING FOR KOREA

KINCH ARRIVED in Seoul, Korea, in September, 1951, just about a year later than he had thought he would be there. It had been an impatient year of training and more training, and a brief but unexciting fling at test-pilot work.

Despite the urgency of the Korean "police action," the Air Force was not sending raw rookies fresh out of flying school into combat, not even "hot" rookies like Iven Kincheloe, so Kinch had to swallow his eagerness for combat and plod through the routine of advanced tactical training.

After a brief stay at Selfridge Air Force Base, the home of Gabreski's 56th Fighter Group, Kinch was sent to O'Hare Air Force Base in Chicago to the 62nd Fighter Interceptor Squadron, one of three squadrons which made up the 56th. There he was a"checked out" on a new type of airplane, the North American F-86 Sabre.

The F-86 was a single-seat jet fighter, at that time the most advanced in Air Force service. It had a top speed of 650 miles an hour, a good hundred miles an hour faster than the jet trainers Kinch had flown at Williams. It had a terrific rate of climb and a very high degree of maneuverability.

Kinch felt the F-86 had been designed especially for him; it was *the* airplane. As he had in the past, he studied every detail of the Sabre and its engine, and in flight he put the swept-wing jet through every maneuver in the book and a couple of new ones he invented.

The training program at O'Hare was like an advanced repetition of his course at Williams. Starting with the early solos in the F-86, Kinch progressed over the months through aerobatics, instrument work, and formation flying. In ground school he learned about engineering and maintenance of the Sabre, new techniques of combat flying which were being employed in Korea, the daily intelligence picture of the progress of the war, the role of the fighter-interceptor in action, and methods of survival and escape in the event he should be shot down over enemy territory. At all of it Kinch worked overtime. He wanted to be a combat pilot so badly he could taste it, but more than that he wanted to be a *live* combat pilot, for to Kinch the career-planner, Korea and the decorations it might bring were just a step to bigger things.

In early 1951, Kinch progressed to the "meat" of the tactical training course—gunnery and air tactics. It started with air-to-ground gunnery, making high-speed passes at ground targets firing the F-86's six .50 caliber machine guns and the eight underwing rockets. Next came air-to-air gunnery, firing at a sleeve target towed by another high-speed plane. Then, finally, simulated combat or "dogfighting," in which one F-86 would play the part of a Communist MIG-15 and another would attempt to shoot it down, the results being measured by gun cameras.

To Iven Kincheloe this was *real* flying. It demanded the utmost skill to dive and twist and maneuver the hot F-86 into position to line up the gun sights long enough to register camera hits. It had the thrill of danger, because there was always the chance of collision as the planes rolled all over the sky in violent maneuvers; it had the feel of authentic combat flying; and it had the zest of competition as the "enemy" pilot dodged to stay out of the camera sights.

Kinch was good at the dogfighting phase of the training program, but he was dismayed to find he was not as good as he thought he would be. He had excellent eyesight, and he could spot the "enemy" plane as soon as anyone, usually about three miles away. But in a head-on attack the combined speed of the two airplanes was such that it took less than ten seconds to close the gap, and the "enemy" was whipping by at incredible speed. Then came the hard work of giving chase and trying to close on the other airplane, an extremely difficult job since both planes had identical performance, and a strenuous one because of the bodily strain in high "G" climbs and turns. There was a big thrill of accomplishment when the gun cameras recorded hits, but it was a thrill which came all too infrequently.

By this time, Kinch was flying the F-86 with near-perfect precision, as though he and the airplane were one integral piece of machinery. He could make the speedy Sabre do just about anything he wanted it to do, but he was learning that there was more to combat flying than handling the airplane. You had to outthink the other guy, figure out what he was going to do next and then short-cut him to get into strike position. Kinch concentrated on the "thinking game" for weeks and found it paid off. His camera kills were picking up and his confidence curve started upward again. Then, suddenly, the preparations for Korea were interrupted by a new assignment.

The Air Research and Development Command wanted a

regular, operational pilot from a line squadron to do a special test job on the F-86. The 62nd Squadron, one of the few in the United States with F-86 equipment, was called upon to provide the pilot, and Kinch got the nod. He was placed on detached duty and sent to the Air Force Flight Test Center at Edwards Air Force Base in California's Mojave Desert.

Kinch went to Edwards with mixed emotions. He felt the test assignment would delay his eagerly awaited tour of combat in Korea. On the other hand, he would be a test pilot, even if only a junior-grade one and only for a few weeks. It would be on his record, and that might help when he returned from Korea and applied for test-pilot school, a plan he had already formulated.

The test job turned out to be a very routine operation. It was called a Phase VI test, and it consisted of flying a great many hours in as short a time as possible on a new version of the Sabre called the F-86E. He was to check out new armament and other new equipment on the plane on missions similar to those he had been flying at O'Hare.

The work was not particularly interesting, but the test base itself fascinated Iven Kincheloe. Research history was in the making at Edwards. On the flight line, undergoing prototype tests, were a number of new airplanes of incredible performance capabilities, planes which would not be in line service for years. And there were the special research aircraft, the "X" series, rocket jobs like the X-1A and the Skystreak, which could fly faster in a steep climb than Kinch's Sabre could in a dive. These planes were probing new frontiers of speed and altitude and to Iven Kincheloe, test pilot junior grade, just looking at them and touching their sleek skins was something akin to a child's first meeting with Santa Claus. The thrill was heightened by meeting the great test pilots—Yeager, Everest, Bridgeman, Crossfield—Kincheloe idols all.

Kinch spent every free minute he could find on the flight line, inspecting the magnificent planes, plying the engineers with questions, watching take-offs and landings, peering over the shoulders of the maintenance men as they took the great airplanes apart. This, he knew, was something he had to become a part of, a prober into the unknown areas of flight.

All too quickly, the F-86E Phase VI test was concluded. He had done a good job, the engineers told him, and he glowed with satisfaction. It had been a very worth-while experience, he decided. He knew more than he ever had about the Sabre and how to fly it, and that could not help but pay off in Korea. More than that, he had had a glimpse of the greatest operation in aeronautics, the Air Force Flight Test Center.

He returned to O'Hare in late summer of 1951 and found that his tour at Edwards had not delayed his projected combat service one iota. The 62nd Squadron was still there, its pilots chafing at the bit. They were beginning to wonder if there really was a war in Korea, and if there was, why in the hell were they not being permitted to get into it?

Kinch settled back into the routine of advanced tactical training, more impatient than ever. The sooner he got into combat and out of it, the sooner he could apply for test-pilot school. Combat was only an interim step in the Master Plan.

His old college roommate, Rex Sebastian, was getting married on the first of September and Kinch had consented to be best man. He drove into Chicago to buy a civilian suit for the occasion. Returning to the squadron that afternoon, he got the great news—he was going to Korea! The squadron was not going as a unit, but a few of the more combat-ready men had been selected as replacement pilots. Kinch was at the top of the list. The big moment he had feared would never come was here at last.

VI. IVEN KINCHELOE, DOUBLE ACE

THE KOREAN winter was issuing the first warnings of its approach when Kinch reported to Kimpo Air Base near Seoul in early September of 1951. In a place like Korea, the old hands told him, winter didn't make much difference; things just went from miserable to lousy.

Kinch didn't think it miserable. He was, after all, in the combat zone at last, and living conditions, while far from Waldorf-style, were not so bad. He was assigned quarters in a big, open-bay barracks which he shared with eleven other pilots. It had a few windows, an indoor shower and latrine, and a potbellied stove, and Kinch felt it might have been a lot worse. He also shared a houseboy, a little ten-year-old Korean named Kim, who cleaned his clothes, shined his shoes, swept up his bunk area, kept his foot locker in orderly condition, and did anything else he was asked for twelve thousand *won* a month, or two American dollars. The food you couldn't call good, but it was adequate.

His outfit was the 325th Fighter Interceptor Squadron of the 4th Fighter Wing. It was equipped with F-86 Sabres and manned by a combination of young pilots like himself (he was now twenty-three) and "old-timers" from World War II, some of whom had stayed in the Air Force after the war and others who had drifted back from civilian life with the outbreak of hostilities in Korea.

Kinch spent his first week getting briefed on the tactical situation.

The role of the fighter-interceptor in Korea, he learned, was for the most part flying escort for other Air Force planes—the Lockheed RF-80 reconnaissance planes and the Republic F-84 fighter-bombers based farther to the south in Korea, and the Boeing B-29 bombers based in Japan. In addition, the 325th flew fighter "sweeps" to seek out and destroy as many enemy aircraft as possible.

The competition, the Chinese Communists or "Chicoms," was flying mainly the Russian-built MIG-15, a jet which bore a marked resemblance to the F-86 in general configuration, but which was smaller and lighter and had superior high-altitude performance. They operated from bases in Manchuria.

The battleground for the jet air war, "MIG Alley" as it was called, was an area in the northwest corner of the Korean peninsula between the Yalu River, the borderline between Manchuria and North Korea, and the Chongchon River, which ran roughly parallel to the Yalu some seventy-five miles to the south. The major center of action was in the vicinity of the Manchurian city of Antung and the Korean town of Sinuiju just across the Yalu at the point where the river empties into the Yellow Sea. From Kimpo Air Base, or K-14 as it was called in the United Nations geographical code, it was about 250 miles to Antung.

The fighter-interceptor wings had developed a new set of tactics for Korean operations. The mass-formation flights of World War II had been abandoned. In their stead, the Air

Force flew in four-plane flights called "fluid fours." The flight consisted of two elements of two planes each: in the lead element was the flight leader and his "wing man," who flew at the same altitude and slightly behind the leader. The second element, consisting of leader and wing man, flew five hundred to one thousand feet higher and behind the lead element. The two element leaders were ordinarily the "shooters," who dived to attack while the wing men covered them; the wing men were the "lookers," who continually scanned the sky for sight of the enemy and, in particular, watched for surprise attacks from the rear and above. In practice, all members of the flight watched everywhere with "swivel necks" and the wing men as well as the element leaders sometimes became "shooters."

The fluid-four formation had a lot of advantages over the big formation. It helped prevent the surprise attack, because the four-plane flight presented a smaller radar target. It provided greater maneuverability, because the planes were not in each other's way. It permitted greater speed, since in a large formation lower-speed operation was required so as not to produce "stragglers." And it allowed greater coverage of the battle zone, by breaking up the squadron into small units, each of which covered a given area.

If Kinch had hoped to blow a lot of MIGs out of the sky in his first few weeks in Korea, the series of briefings chilled his enthusiasm. MIG kills, he found, happened "very seldom."

Because of the battle situation, the advantages were all on the side of the Chicoms. Operating from Manchuria, they were safe from ground attack because of an official directive which prohibited U.N. forces from crossing the Yalu, one which was flagrantly disobeyed in the jet air war by pilots who "lost their bearings" in the heat of battle. The target zone was, of course, in North Korea, so the Chicoms had the whole area blanketed with ground radar. The prevailing winds were from the northwest, which meant that the F-86's had to buck them en route to the battle zone. They had to carry extra fuel in cumbersome external fuel tanks, dropping the tanks when battle was joined, thereby limiting the time they could fight, since they had to keep enough fuel to fly the two hundred or more miles back to home base. On top of all this, the Chicoms enjoyed numerical superiority in jets.

There were other difficulties in getting kills. For one thing, the Chicoms were rarely eager to fight. They would engage the F-86's briefly, forcing them to drop the tip tanks, then turn and head across the Yalu. On the rare occasions when they became aggressive, they still had the edge, because their MIGs were more maneuverable at high altitude. The kills usually came only when the American pilots, who had a conceded edge in flying skill and training, were able to coax unwary adversaries down to a favorable altitude. Generally speaking, the "gutless" Chicom pilot who wanted to go home alive could do so by exploiting all his advantages.

Still, there were days when the Chicoms, perhaps prompted by orders from the high command to "get in there and fight," would seek out the battle. These were the days the American fighter pilots looked for, because, like Kinch, most of them were eager for kills. "Every man a tiger!"—that was their motto.

Kinch flew five missions in the month of September and all he got out of them was an indoctrination in the geography of North Korea. Flying as wing man to the flight leader, he flew the first two without ever seeing an enemy airplane. On the third, ranging northeast from Sinuiju near the Yalu, his flight spotted the vapor trails of a MIG formation flying high above them and headed in the opposite direction. It was not an "eager day" for the Chicoms. They made a slow, sweep-

43

ing turn to the north and slipped across the Yalu. The fourth and fifth missions were like the first two—"milk runs," with not a single Chicom contrail to mar the peaceful blue of the North Korean sky.

Kinch's comments on the guts of the Chinese Communist Air Force were violent. He saw his dreams of combat heroics evaporating in a mist of Chicom cowardice. The standard combat tour for a U.S.A.F. pilot was one hundred missions, a mission being a sortie across the thirty-eighth parallel of latitude into territory held by the enemy. He had already flown one-twentieth of them and he had not been close enough to a Chicom airplane to make out its configuration.

Slowly becoming resigned to the dullness of combat, he flew two more uneventful missions in early October. Then, as the Korean winter warmed up to its job, the weather closed down and for a couple of weeks there was no flying activity. Late in the month, on his tenth mission, he got his first slight taste of action.

The flight was north of Anju at the mouth of the Chong-chon River when Kinch spotted a trio of MIGs, coming fast from the west. He called them out over the radio and the four F-86's turned to do battle. The flight leader banked to a cutoff path and dove at the trailing MIG, Kinch right behind him covering. The MIG trio turned to a new heading, northward, and started to climb. They headed straight for the Yalu and it was immediately apparent that the F-86's could not overtake them. Far out of range, Kinch triggered a burst from his guns in exasperation.

By mid-November, Kinch had racked up sixteen missions. He had not even recorded a damage claim. On two occasions, he had been able to "mix it" in brief passes at the Chicoms, but he had not got close enough in either battle to fire a telling burst.

Then came the word he was to be transferred to a new outfit, and to Kinch it was great news. His old boss from Selfridge, famed World War II ace Colonel Francis "Gabby" Gabreski, had arrived in Korea to form a new wing. A number of the pilots from the 4th Fighter were being shifted to Gabby's unit and Kinch had been selected as one of them.

Kinch moved on November 15. The move was a short one, fifteen miles down the road from Kimpo to Suwon, a small town just a few miles from the Yellow Sea coastline. Gabreski's wing, which was being equipped with F-86E's, was the 51st Fighter Wing, and it was based at Suwon Air Base or K-13. The wing had two squadrons, the 16th and 25th. Kinch was assigned to the latter.

Suwon was a desolate village consisting of a few rows of huts and a ramshackle railroad station. The villagers were thin and hungry, dirty and ragged, and some of the children were naked, even in the Korean winter. The stench, so characteristic of all of South Korea, was perhaps one degree more noticeable in Suwon than it had been at Kimpo.

K-13 was located about five miles from the village, and although it was hardly elaborate, it seemed luxurious by comparison. The runways and taxiways were pierced steel planks laid atop Korean mud. Around the edge of the field, the planes were parked on individual planked stands ringed by sandbag revetments. There were several maintenance hangars spread along the inner edge of the field; they were of the lean-to variety, with sandbag walls. There was a U-shaped wooden operations building and near it the control tower, a small wooden shack on stilt legs.

The living quarters were similar to those at Kimpo. The 25th Fighter Interceptor Squadron housing area was a long double row of corrugated iron barracks on either side of a brick walk. Kinch shared one of these "shacks" with ten

45

other pilots, including two of his closest friends, Curtis "Dad" Eskew and Dale Smiley, both lieutenants.

The most comfortable building on the base, aside from "Gabreski's Palace," a wooden bungalow, was the Officers' Club. The club, U-shaped like the operations building, was constructed of corrugated iron. One half of the U was the dining hall; the other, more important half was the bar, furnished with rattan furniture scrounged from Japan.

Kinch spent most of his off-duty time in the bar, not that he was a heavy drinker, but there were always people there and he loved to talk and listen. He had a natural flair for storytelling, and he would recount by the hour the brief engagements in which he had participated, diving, rolling, and climbing with hand gestures, interspersing the narrative with witty comment, exaggerating everything until the tamest milk run sounded like one of the great air battles of history.

When he was not in a talkative mood, Kinch liked to listen, and he would prod the World War II vets into retelling stories he had heard a number of times. Characteristically, Kinch sought out these older and more experienced pilots. He was "hot" and he knew it, but he also knew that these men could teach him a lot about flying, and he never tired of learning more about his art.

At K-13, there was a wealth of experienced talent for Kinch to pump. There was Gabreski, of course, a friendly, affable guy who didn't act like a colonel but who could be very "hard-nosed" when he had to be. Gabby had been drawn to the big, cheerful blond youngster from the first time they met, when Kinch had reported to Gabby's wing at Selfridge. Gabby had visited the Kincheloe farm at Cassopolis with Kinch a couple of times, and the two had become close friends despite the C.O.-junior officer relationship. Gabby liked Kinch's fast wit and booming laugh, his easy personality, and most of all, his intense devotion to the Air Force and to flying. To Kinch, the great ace was a living idol.

Kinch, always the hero-worshiper, had a number of other idols at K-13. There were Colonel Walker "Bud" Mahurin and Colonel Al Schinz, both top aces from the earlier war, and Lieutenant Colonel George L. Jones, Gabby's group commander, the group being the operational portion of the wing. There was Curt Utterback, a captain, Major Bill Westcott, and Elmer "Hap" Harris, a World War II vet and an airline pilot who had been recalled for a Korean tour as a major.

Two of the closest idols were the two squadron commanders. Major Don Adams had been with Kinch at Selfridge and O'Hare and had led an aerobatic team of which Kinch had been a member. At K-13, he commanded the 16th Fighter Interceptor Squadron. Bill Whisner, also a major and commander of Kinch's 25th Squadron, was one of Kinch's closest friends. They had been together from Selfridge to Kimpo to Suwon.

At the frequent beer-and-cheese parties in the club, or over a post-mission coffee, Kinch would pick the brains of all these vets, as if he were trying to absorb their combined experience in his own mind and body. When he was not brain-picking, he studied manuals on combat tactics by the hour, and roamed the maintenance line, asking questions and filing the answers away in his storehouse of aeronautical knowledge. Whenever an accident occurred, Kinch would conduct his own private investigation. What had happened? Why had the engine flamed out? What could be done to prevent a recurrence? He would run the details of the accident through his computer-like mind and decide how he would handle the same situation if it happened to him. The driving ambition and the insatiable thirst for knowledge were still with him.

Sometimes, over coffee, he would confide to Gabby or Bill Whisner his plans for the future. He would tell them of the things he had seen in his brief tour at Edwards and outline his career plan for becoming a part of the research and development effort. They encouraged him to keep at it, for Kinch was a pilot who stood out from the crowd and both knew he had what it took to be a great test pilot.

From the time he joined the 51st, the action in Korea picked up. The Chicoms were in an aggressive mood, and they had been joined by highly skilled Russian pilots. Kinch flew four missions in the first two weeks of December in his new F-86E, which he had named "Ivan." On all four he saw action and on one he scored his first damage claim. He executed a neat cutoff on a MIG, got in close enough for an opening burst, and stuck to the tail of the Chicom pilot through a wild series of maneuvers, firing burst after burst. He saw his tracers slam into the wing of the MIG and he watched, hopefully, for the explosion. But the MIG wriggled away and set sail for the Yalu. Kinch could not catch him.

He had twenty missions now and still no kills, but he had learned a lot about combat tactics and his confidence was high. He felt that any mission he would score.

Bill Whisner, the squadron commander, gave Kinch a Christmas present: he was named flight commander of "B" flight. Although they flew in fours, the flight had eight pilots. Dad Eskew was one of them; another was Joe Cannon, who had been with Kinch through most of his flying career. Then there were Harry Shumate, R. J. Koenig, Frank Gately, Jim Ross, and Bill Guinther, all lieutenants.

January was a big action month for the 51st. The weather was good and they were flying every day, sometimes twice a day. On the sixth, the 51st tangled with a big force of MIGs near Antung and four pilots, including Bud Mahurin and

John Heard from the 25th, scored kills. Kinch's "B" flight tallied three damage hits, Kinch getting one of them and Eskew and Guinther the others. It was the wing's most successful day and it was duly noted by a wild victory party at the club, during which the furniture suffered slight damage when "B" flight challenged a flight from the 16th Squadron to an indoor football game.

The next day, Kinch took Colonel Bud Mahurin aside and asked for advice.

"I'm flying as well as anyone," he said, "but all I can score is damage. What am I doing wrong?"

Mahurin agreed to study Kinch's flying and Kinch, who was now also assistant operations officer, assigned Bud to his own flight for the next day's mission. They got a "tangle" above the Chongchon and Kinch dove for a kill, Mahurin covering on his wing. The MIG got away, but Mahurin had diagnosed the trouble.

Back at K-13, as they strolled off the flight line, Mahurin re-created the action.

"You boxed him nicely and you should have had him, Kinch. But you were too eager and you fired too soon. You were so far out of range it was ridiculous." Kinch nodded thoughtfully. That was probably it. Together they studied the gun-camera film, which proved Mahurin right; the tracers were dropping behind the enemy plane. It was an important lesson for Kinch.

That week Kinch made another new friend, one who proved valuable later in Kinch's career. Major Don Rodewald was a Pentagon officer who had come over to investigate a problem with the automatic gunsight. He would fly a dozen missions with the 51st.

They met in the club and when Rodewald had outlined his assignment, Kinch plunged into a pumping session to learn all about gunsights. Later, Kinch fixed it so Rodewald could fly his tour with "B" flight.

The twenty-fifth of January was another big day for the 51st and *the* big day for Iven Kincheloe. He was leading the flight of four, heading east toward Anju, when Gately, on his wing, called the "bounce." Below and directly ahead of them there were three MIGs, moving at moderate cruise speed. Kinch, with the sun behind him, had the element of surprise. Pushing down the nose of the F-86, he started a screaming dive toward the right wingman of the MIG flight. He closed rapidly, right on the MIG's tail, pulling in to within eight hundred feet before the startled MIG pilot discovered his peril. The MIG started an evasive turn, but it was too late. Kinch let go with his .50 calibers, watched the tracers hit the MIG from wing tip to tip. Parts of the wing flew off, the MIG snapped out of control and then disappeared in a great ball of flame and smoke. Kinch had his first kill, the 340th MIG destroyed by American jets in the Korean war.

Gately and Guinther also scored that day as the squadron racked up a five-kill tally. Three of the five had been knocked out of the sky by "B" flight. There was a great victory party, and Kinch told the story over and over until, as someone said, he got "finger fatigue" from flying with his hands.

On the thirtieth, he got more good news. He received a spot field promotion to captain, another step on the ladder.

It had been a big month for the 51st. The 25th Squadron had flown 496 sorties and had blasted fifteen MIGs. Kinch had scored four damages in addition to his kill; he had flown twenty-five missions for a total of fifty-five. Bill Whisner and Gabby Gabreski had each destroyed two. It was not all gravy, though; three pilots of the 51st had been shot down during the month.

February started off like another big month for Iven Kincheloe. On the second, flying an escort mission with Joe Cannon on his wing, he spotted a lone MIG and dove for it. He scored hits on the first pass, but the MIG did not go down. Kinch wheeled his F-86 in a tight turn and made another pass. The MIG started a steep climbing turn, seeking the safety of altitude, but Kinch cut inside him, moved in close, and triggered another burst. Suddenly, the MIG's canopy flew off and the Chicom pilot followed it out of the cockpit. Kinch and Cannon both yelled as they saw the 'chute billow out and then, as they watched the crippled MIG plunge earthward, Kinch spotted another one about three thousand feet below them.

"Go get him, Joe," he shouted. "It's your turn."

Cannon rolled over and dived at the MIG, letting go a long burst as he moved into range. A streak of flame shot out from the MIG and its wing tip flew off. "B" flight had scored two kills within a minute. And suddenly, Kinch was shouting into the radio:

"Break right, Joe! Break right!"

An unseen MIG had crept right up on Cannon's tail pipe, and he was shooting. The bullets slammed into the canopy, through the instrument panel, and into the fuselage, miraculously missing Cannon. A tongue of flame was licking at the wing root of Cannon's Sabre.

Someone in another plane yelled.

"Bail out, Joe!"

"Shut up!" came Kinch's sharp voice. It was Cannon's decision.

Despite the fire, Cannon decided to stay with it. They were still deep in enemy territory and a bail-out unquestionably meant internment for the rest of the war. They headed south and flew in silence for ten agonizing minutes, Kinch flying

Cannon's wing, nervously watching the fire. The plane could explode at any second.

Still behind enemy lines, Cannon made his decision. He released the shattered canopy, pulled the ejection handle, and blew himself out of the cockpit. Kinch circled as the 'chute descended, fearful lest some MIGs should be lurking in the area, then, as Cannon dropped to the ground, he turned sadly for Suwon.

Lucky Joe Cannon evaded a dozen Communist patrols and walked through the enemy lines in two days. He walked into the 51st club on the second night and got a wild pummeling and shouting reception. Kinch lifted him clean off the floor and almost cracked a rib in a bear hug, then announced that Cannon had been on vacation long enough and he would schedule the returnee for a dawn mission. He was overruled by the flight surgeon.

That same week, Kinch became involved in an incident that had top-level repercussions. One night he was alone in his barracks, writing letters home and listening to the radio. Actually, he was listening to a program which had been tape-recorded by his friends Eskew and Smiley, although he didn't know it.

Suddenly, the "announcer" broke into the music.

"We interrupt this program," he said, "to bring you a special announcement. News just received from Panmunjom advises that the war is over. I repeat—the war is now officially over."

Kinch leaped to his feet, charged out the door, falling over a bicycle, and ran to Bill Whisner's room.

"Maje!" he shouted. "Maje! The war's over. I just heard it on the radio. I knew it. I knew it, dammit. They beat me out of those other three MIGs."

Whisner, who had not been in on the joke, sent squadron

exec Curt Utterback in search of Gabreski. Gabreski, who had missions scheduled for the morning, called to 5th Air Force Headquarters for confirmation. The duty officer there had heard nothing, of course; but he started a check of his own superiors. The practical joke had the whole Air Force in an uproar and Gabreski's face was somewhat red when the word came back from the top that someone was pulling his leg. He ordered Whisner to conduct a thorough investigation but somehow the investigation stalled out.

February and March slipped by in a period of hectic activity. The air war was hotter than ever. The 25th flew 604 sorties in February and 751 in March. On the twenty-third of February, Bill Whisner became the 51st Wing's first ace, with his fifth kill. Gabby Gabreski became the second a week later.

Kinch generously passed up a chance at his third MIG in late February. Don Rodewald, his gunsight investigation completed, was flying his last mission before returning to Washington to report. They saw a lone MIG cutting across their flight path.

"You're on target, Maje," Kinch called. "Go get him." Rodewald got him. As they headed for home, Kinch said:

"I just couldn't let you go back to that Pentagon without one MIG."

March was a dull month for Kinch. He flew sixteen missions for a total of seventy-one, but only on one or two occasions did he get close enough for a burst. He couldn't even score a damage. He was galled by the fact that one of the younger pilots, Lieutenant Bob Moore of the 16th Squadron, Kinch's classmate and competitor, had become the wing's third ace.

On the last night of the month, he sought out Gabreski in the club.

"I've been doing some homework, boss," he said. "You want to get some MIGs tomorrow?" Gabby didn't have to answer that.

Talking swiftly, Kinch outlined his plan. Contrails, a white stream of vapor caused by mixture of the hot jet exhaust with the cold upper air, normally gave away the position of an attacking airplane before the enemy could spot the plane itself. At times, however, the pilots of the 51st would encounter thin layers of air where contrails did not develop because of unusual temperature conditions. These conditions usually lasted for days at a time.

"I tried it out today," Kinch said. "At thirty-two thousand feet, we got the contrails. But I went up to thirty-eight, and between there and thirty-nine there weren't any. When I went higher than that, the contrails formed again."

Gabby saw the plan clearly now, but he listened while Kinch talked on. Put the main formation at the lower altitude, Kinch suggested, so that their contrails would be clearly visible to the Chicoms. Another group would fly higher, in the no-trail zone, and as the Chicoms moved to attack the main formation, the high flight could dive to a surprise attack.

Gabby bought the plan. The next morning, he led twenty-six Sabres to an area south of the Yalu River along the Manchurian border. With Kinch leading the second element, Gabby led a flight of four up at the no-contrail level. The remainder of the wing, in a single formation, flew several thousand feet below, their streaming vapor trails announcing their position.

The Chicoms took the bait. Up high, Gabby and Kinch watched as a large group formed across the river and headed for the main section of the 51st. Gabby waited until they were directly beneath him, then shouted, "Let's go!"

Kinch picked out his "pigeon" and dropped straight at him

in a near-vertical dive, picking up terrific speed. On his first pass, his bullets thudded into the fuselage of the MIG, directly below the cockpit. The aircraft spun out of control and the pilot left it.

Barely giving the stricken pilot a glance, Kinch pulled around sharply, picked out another MIG and dove again. He scored hits on the first pass, wheeled around for another, and overshot. He turned again and caught up with the MIG, his tracers lashing out in an orange streak. Part of the MIG's tail came off and the plane rolled over on its back, then plunged earthward, spinning dizzily, the pilot still in it. Kinch had scored a double kill within a few minutes; he was now just one shy of becoming an ace.

Kinch's strategy had worked beautifully. In all, the 51st got seven MIGs that day and damaged a couple of others. Gabby had made one of the kills.

Later that same week, Kinch scored his fifth. It came on the sixth of April. "B" flight, along with five others, was escorting a group of F-84 fighter bombers on a railroad-busting mission just south of the Yalu, Kinch leading the whole formation. Suddenly, someone called the "bounce." There were a dozen MIGs below and ahead of them, patrolling the river.

Kinch rolled out into the dive and flew "right up the tail pipe" of the rear MIG. He scored hits with a long burst. The MIG started violent evasive maneuvers, dropping lower. Kinch stayed with him, trying to line him up in the sight. The MIG pilot tried a new tactic—he slammed on his dive brakes and slowed rapidly, hoping Kinch would overshoot. But Kinch diagnosed the maneuver in time, and instantly dropped his own brakes. The MIG spiraled down, alternately slowing and diving in a frenzied effort to shake Kinch. For five minutes Kinch chased the Chicom up and down the valley, flying superbly, forcing the MIG lower and lower. Then, when they were just over the tops of the hills, he anticipated the MIG's next slowdown, ignored it, and dove straight at the Chicom, picking up speed and moving in right on the MIG's tail. He triggered his guns and held the button down for a long burst. He flipped into a tight bank as he shot over the MIG, and over his shoulder he saw the enemy plane roll over on its back and smash into the ground upside down. He was an ace, the fourth in the wing, the tenth in almost two years of Korean air war.

It was a great "ace party" that night at the club. Everyone from Gabreski to the lowest line mechanic, knowing the intensity of Kinch's yearning to make the select ace category, had been rooting for him, and now that he had made it, a real celebration was called for. Around the walls of the club there were posters ribbing Kinch about his prominent ears, his "hand-talking," and his brain-picking. There was liquor and beer and cheese and pretzels and pandemonium. Kinch made a speech, sympathizing with his fellow pilots who had not made ace and who could now never make the first ten, the only ones who really counted. Everyone said it was the greatest ace party ever.

Shortly thereafter, Kinch got a few days off. He took a plane to Japan for maintenance and at the big Tachikawa overhaul base had a reunion with two old flying-school buddies, D. D. "Dolph" Overton and Russ Harmon. Harmon was flying transports out of Tachikawa; Overton was in F-84 fighter-bombers flying from a Korean base far south of K-13. They discovered that Kinch had flown escort for Overton, and this touched off some banter as to which was the more important assignment. Kidding Kinch, Overton said that anyone could become a jet ace, but that low-level bombing took real skill. This drew a big blast from Kinch, who allowed that fighter bomber pilots were just truck drivers.

56

"Kinch," said Overton, "I think I'll transfer to those F-86's and shoot down five of those MIGs in a week or so and then get out of this Air Force and go back to South Carolina." Kinch, who had needed eighty-four missions to get his five kills, just smiled. Unbelievably, Overton lived up to his brash boast. With Kinch's help, he transferred to F-86's after completing 101 missions in the fighter-bombers. After flying forty-five missions without a score, and learning, perhaps, the reason for Kinch's smile, he suddenly became the hottest pilot in the Air Force, shot down five MIGs in four days for an all-time Korean kill record, then returned home and resigned from the Air Force.

Later in the month, Kinch got another MIG in the air, and in addition, a YAK-9 on the ground. The YAK-9 was an old piston-engine fighter rarely seen in action. On a surveillance mission above the Chongchon, with Elmer "Hap" Harris on his wing, Kinch spotted two YAKs parked on the apron of a small air base. It was rare to see an enemy plane on the ground in Korea, since the MIGs were all based in Manchuria. Kinch couldn't resist the temptation, although strafing was not part of his assignment. He and Harris buzzed the field several times, pouring burst after burst into the two YAKs and completely destroying them.

In May, fighting activity fell off as the MIGs, who had taken a terrific pasting in the first four months of 1952, became more and more reluctant to engage in combat. They no longer ventured across the Yalu except on rare occasions; they were content to cruise around in the safety of Manchuria and look threatening. Their timidity was justifiable; the U.S.A.F. had rolled up a score of fourteen MIG kills for every F-86 lost.

Mindful of his earlier discovery of the YAK, Kinch would go ground-hunting when it became apparent that there would

57

be no MIG action. During his last dozen missions in May, he found three more and destroyed them, giving him a grand total of ten planes destroyed, eleven damaged, and making him a double ace.

Then, in mid-May, it was all over. His last mission was as uneventful as his first—not a sign of an enemy. He landed at K-13 and gave "Ivan," his airplane, a last pat on the nose. It had been a great tour; he had done even better than he had hoped. He was going home with a whole chestful of ribbons: a Silver Star for his great double kill on April 1, a Distinguished Flying Cross, the Air Medal with two oak-leaf clusters, the Korean Service Medal with three bronze stars, a Distinguished Unit Citation Emblem, the Republic of Korea Presidential Unit Citation, and the United Nations Service Medal.

His initial assignment on return to the United States was to be gunnery instructor at Nellis Air Force Base, Nevada. He wouldn't be there long, he felt. He would apply for test pilot as soon as he got there, and with his aeronautical-engineering degree, his demonstrated flying ability, and his well-publicized war record, it should be a cinch.

VII. FRUSTRATION AT NELLIS AFB

THE FIRST couple of weeks after Kinch returned stateside were good ones. As a Korean double ace, he got considerable attention from the press. His picture and stories about his combat work were carried in papers from coast to coast and from Cassopolis to Las Vegas, his new home. Kinch did not let the publicity go to his head, but he had to admit that he liked it. What youngster of twenty-three wouldn't? It had its practical side, too; Kinch felt that the newspaper and magazine articles would call top-level Air Force attention to him and help ease his way into test-pilot school.

He checked into Nellis Air Force Base, where he was to be a fighter-gunnery instructor with the 3596th Flying Training Squadron. It was old home week; there were a lot of Korean vets already at Nellis, among them Major Bill Wescott from the 25th Squadron, Captain Bob Moore, Kinch's old competitor who had beaten him to ace rank, and Captain Dave Freeland, whom Kinch had first met at Perrin, known later at Williams, and most recently in Korea, where Dave had been assigned to the 16th Squadron.

59

The letdown started shortly after he reported to Nellis. First he was demoted, stripped of his spot combat promotion to captain and dropped back to first lieutenant. This was a not infrequent occurrence, since the Air Force, operating on a peacetime table of organization despite the war in Korea, did not have enough captaincies to go around and in May of 1952 Iven Kincheloe still had less than three years of commissioned service. To Kinch it was an awful blow, a backward step as far as his career plan was concerned. He felt it was no way to treat a double ace.

And he did not care for the work. He was assigned a group of raw jet pilots fresh from Williams and told to teach them combat gunnery. Among the group, only one or two had any flying ability and Kinch was impatient with the others. A near-perfect pilot himself, he could not understand why the rookies were unable to do things which to him were second nature. Because they were slow to learn, he felt he was a poor instructor.

The publicity in which he had reveled turned out to be a minus instead of a plus. A couple of his superiors in the gunnery school, men who had wanted to go to Korea but had never made it, resented the tall, good-looking, wisecracking double ace, and he came in for what he considered unfair needling.

As he had planned, he applied for test-pilot school. The routine months dragged on and he heard nothing about his application. The test-pilot ranks were hard to crash; only sixteen trainees from the whole Air Force were accepted for each course. All applicants had to be aeronautical engineers, so he had no edge there, but he felt that there could not be too many young pilots who had amassed the number of flying hours that he had, and certainly there were not very many double aces. What had happened? He had a suspicion that, because of the petty jealousies on the part of his superiors, the application had never left the base. The Iven Kincheloe career program was wobbling; his drive and ambition were ebbing because of insufficient fuel.

He consoled himself by piling up a great many flying hours, which might help if the people "upstairs" ever got a look at his application. Nellis was a good place to accumulate time. With his gunnery trainees he flew six or seven missions a day in F-86's. In his off-time, he haunted the operations office, begging to "check out" on every plane on the base, and he took all the cross-country flights he could get.

When he was not flying, he was a frequent visitor to the night spots of the Vegas "Strip." Handsome as a movie star, famous to a degree, and full of personality, he was a popular favorite with Vegas' female colony. To entertain them properly, he bought a big, black convertible Cadillac with money he had saved from Korea. He and Bob Moore made a number of trips to Los Angeles, which was only a few hundred miles away.

On one such trip, he visited the test center at Edwards Air Force Base, a hundred miles from Los Angeles. He looked up a couple of the top test pilots, Major Stuart Childs and Lieutenant Colonel Frank "Pete" Everest. Everest was chief of flight test, and at that time the Air Force's number-one test pilot, "Chuck" Yeager having been reassigned to an operational flying job. He told Childs and Everest of his great longing to become a test pilot, and they listened with interest. Everest suggested that Kinch apply again, and said that if necessary, he would put in a letter requesting Kinch's transfer.

Back at Nellis, his hopes rising, Kinch applied again for test-pilot training. Nothing happened. The months went by.

In April, 1953, the Air Force repromoted Kinch to captain, which restored some of his enthusiasm. A couple of months later, he got another break when he wangled a transfer to the research and development squadron, a unit of the weapons school commanded by his friend Major Bill Westcott. This was test-piloting of a sort, investigating the characteristics of rockets and new gunnery equipment. It was not what he really wanted, but it was a step.

He went to Westcott and told him he wanted to apply once more for test-pilot school. He asked for assurance that it would go through.

"Will you approve it?"

"I sure will," said Bill Westcott.

Still nothing happened. Westcott had approved and forwarded the application. Maybe it had been "shortstopped" on a higher level at Nellis. Maybe the people who screen such applications had just decided that Iven Kincheloe was not a test-pilot type, for reasons he could not fathom.

His spirits reached a new low in the summer of fifty-three. The Korean war had ended in a stalemate and his research and development work on gunnery systems no longer seemed as important as it had. He started to think about revising his career plan.

On his visits to Los Angeles, he had met a number of people from the aircraft-manufacturing companies. Twice he had been offered jobs, as a civilian pilot in their production test operations with a chance to move into the aeronautical-engineering ranks later. The flying would not be spectacular, nothing like the advanced test work at Edwards, not too far removed from what he was doing at Nellis. There was, however, the chance to put his education to better use, there was considerably more money, and there was opportunity to move up the ladder as a civilian. He still loved the Air Force and he hated the thought of resigning, but the future at Nellis looked bleak.

He mulled over the problem for a couple of months, reluctant to start the resignation process. In November, the offer from one of the aircraft companies was repeated. He had to make up his mind quickly.

That week he was assigned an official cross-country to conduct some business at the Pentagon. In Washington, he looked up his old friend Don Rodewald, the Pentagon gunnery expert who had flown with Kinch in Korea. In Rodewald's office, they had a long talk, Kinch pouring out his troubles, Rodewald, now a lieutenant colonel, listening sympathetically.

Kinch concluded by telling of the offer from the manufacturer.

"What do you think, Rodie?" he asked. "Should I get out of the Air Force?"

"I can't answer that, Kinch," Rodewald replied deliberately. "If you got out and found you didn't like civilian life, you'd blame me. It's something you'll just have to decide for yourself."

Kinch got up.

"I wish I could," he said.

When Kinch had left to do his Pentagon errands, Rodewald sat for a long time, thoughtfully staring at the wall. Then he left his desk and went down the hall to the personnel office. To a friend in Personnel, he outlined Kinch's dilemma and asked if there was any chance of getting assigned to the test-pilot school.

The personnel officer shook his head. No, he said, they had just filled the quota for the next class at Edwards.

"Wait a minute, though," he added. "We have an exchange deal with the British where we send two, pilots to their test school. There's a new exchange coming up and we haven't made any assignments. Do you think Kincheloe would like that?"

Like it? Kinch danced on air when Rodewald told him of the possibility. The Empire Test Pilots' School had a solid reputation; it was every bit as good as the U.S.A.F.'s school at Edwards. In addition, there was the luster of training on foreign soil and flying foreign aircraft.

Kinch applied immediately and Rodewald, with the help of his friend in Personnel, was able to push the deal through. The official word came just before Christmas of 1953, the greatest Christmas present Kinch could have received. That night the black Cadillac toured the Vegas strip in celebration. The career program was back on its track. Kinch's debate about leaving the Air Force evaporated in the glorious prospect of becoming a test pilot at last. A chance visit to the Pentagon had changed the whole direction of his life.

VIII. THE EMPIRE TEST PILOTS' SCHOOL

In HIS eagerness to get going on his test-pilot career, Kinch arrived at the Empire Test Pilots' School a week early. The E.T.P.S., as he knew it, was located in the small, typically British town of Farnborough, about forty miles from London.

Farnborough's biggest industry was the Royal Aircraft Establishment, a huge base where the Air Ministry and the Ministry of Supply tested their latest aeronautical products. The E.T.P.S. was just one of many activities at the base. Located in the eastern corner of the airfield, with a separate entrance gate just opposite Farnborough's ancient Queen's Hotel, the E.T.P.S. consisted of the mess, or officers' club, a couple of severe frame classroom buildings, and a flight line with a pair of hangars and a wide variety of aircraft.

The mess was a red-brick building, neatly landscaped but rather austere inside, large enough to house the school staff and the twenty-nine officer pilots who would start No. 13 Course on February 1, 1954. It had a large entrance hall, a dining room, a small receiving lounge, and, at one end of the building, the pub or barroom. The rest of the mess was cut up into small rooms, one for each officer.

As the first to arrive, Kinch got first pick of the rooms and he selected the one directly adjacent to the entrance hallway, opposite another, no more luxurious, occupied by the school commandant, Group Captain Sam Wroath, an affable little Cornishman in his fading forties with curly hair that was also fading.

Later on the day of Kinch's arrival, the second member of No. 13 Course turned up. He was Harry Julian, a lieutenant commander in the Royal Navy. With second choice on rooms, Julian took the one next to Kinch. The two rooms were identical and monotonously drab. Each had an old- fashioned English high bed, a wardrobe, a desk and a single chair, and a tattered rug that might once have been Persian but whose design was now barely distinguishable. The rooms had a wash-stand in one corner and a large window which fronted on the landscaped lawn of the mess. The "facility," as Kinch called it, was down the hall, "within reachable distance in an emergency."

That evening, Kinch was introduced to his batman, Mr. Morley. If Morley had a first name, Kinch never learned it. It was *Mr.* Morley throughout the course. Mr. Morley was wearing what Kinch later discovered was his standard "uniform": a white dress shirt with the sleeves rolled up to the elbow and dark trousers hitched to his bony shoulders by a pair of broad suspenders. Tall and thin, bald with a fringe of gray, his very large nose topped by twinkling blue eyes, Mr. Morley looked and acted like a character out of Dickens. Kinch and his batman took to each other on first sight; they became close friends despite the servant-master relationship.

Kinch also hit it off immediately with Harry Julian, who had as lively a sense of humor as did his new American friend.

Besides flying, they shared a number of common interests, including automobiles. Julian had a unique car, an old Lagonda fitted with a diesel engine taken from a wartime midget submarine, which, as he described it, "was an intriguing mechanical contrivance which gave a modest performance on an infinitesimal fuel consumption." Kinch inspected the car and decided he had to have something like it to get around the area.

Julian had an idea. There were available, he said, a number of old London taxicabs, which were banned from commercial service when they became eighteen years old. They could be bought very inexpensively.

After considering this idea over a couple of beers in the pub, Kinch decided the cab was just the thing.

"Let's go get one," he said. To Iven Kincheloe, tomorrow was always too long to wait; it had to be right now. So he and Julian set off for London in the diesel-powered Lagonda, and after a couple of hours of pub-haunting—the pub seemed the logical place to look—found a cab for sale. The deal with the previous owner was concluded over a couple of pints of ale; Kinch paid over twenty-six pounds, took the keys, christened the vehicle "Lizzie," and drove it back to Farnborough.

"Lizzie" was twenty-five years old but still serviceable. The cab was, as Julian described it later, "the real old kind with a square aspect, spoked wheels, a folding rear quarter to the top, and the most fantastic steering lock ever built. You know the kind I mean, that spin right around in a narrow street and come to a palpitating halt when you raise a suitably rolled umbrella and wave it vigorously."

One by one, the remaining members of No. 13 Course drifted in during the last week in January. They made a conglomerate group, coming as they did from nine different nations—Thailand, Italy, France, The Netherlands, Norway,

Canada, Australia, the United Kingdom, and the United States—and from different branches of the service within those countries.

The other U.S.A.F. representative was Captain R. M. "Dick" Fernbaugh, who brought along a wife named Mike and two children. Fernbaugh had been with the Air Force's all-weather flying laboratory at Wright-Patterson Air Force Base in Dayton, Ohio.

There were two other Americans, both Navy: tall, dark, and handsome Lieutenant F. W. "Bill" Botts, who had been a training instructor at Pensacola, Florida, and Paul Hayek, also a lieutenant, who had been flying with a carrier squadron on the West Coast.

Closest to Kinch, as the acquaintances developed, were Julian and the three Americans, but he also made a number of other fast friends. Among them were Tony Blackman, a flight lieutenant from the Royal Air Force; the two Italians, Commander Riccardo Bignamini and Lieutenant Pietro "Pete" Trevisan; a French pilot, Captain Jean Franchi; Lieutenant Commander J. J. "Jeff" Harvie from the Royal Canadian Navy; and a bubbling little Siamese with an unpronounceable name, Flight Lieutenant Bancha Sukhanusasna, who became simply "Bancho."

No.13 Course started on February 1. It was to last ten months, during which the group would get about 150 hours of actual test-flying experience and several hundred hours of academic instruction on the ground, starting with a "cram" math course and proceeding to such subjects as basic and advanced aerodynamics, aircraft propulsion, stability and control, and, to Kinch, the fascinating new area of rocket power for aircraft. The lectures on these subjects were delivered by school instructors and by top scientists and engineers from the British aircraft industry.

68

Kinch's normal day at the E.T.P.S. went like this:

At precisely 6 A.M., he would be shaken awake by Mr. Morley, who had already laid out Kinch's uniform for the day and had a cup of tea waiting. They played a great game with the tea. Kinch hated it and he would sent Mr. Morley out of the room on any pretext he could think of, then pour the tea down the drain. Mr. Morley knew that Kinch disliked the brew and he knew it was being poured away, but to a traditional Royal Air Force batman it was unthinkable that a pilot should start the day without tea. He would return and pour another cup and stand watching while Kinch grimly sipped some of it.

After breakfast, he would report to the classroom building adjacent to the mess for academics from seven until noon. A break for lunch, then to the flight line, with its varied assemblage of aircraft—jets like the Meteor, Vampire, Hunter, Swift, and Venom; turboprops like the Sea Fury and the Wyvern; a number of older piston-engine types ranging from small private planes to multi-engine bombers; a few helicopters and gliders.

He would be given an assignment to fly one of these planes in a specific series of maneuvers and write a report on his findings. For instance, the instructor would say, "Take up the Meteor and investigate its spin characteristics, then report." The report was more important than the flying; all of the students of Number 13 Course were top pilots, but there was more to being a test pilot than flying. You had to tell the engineers what was wrong and what was right about the airplane you were testing, and you had to do it in clear, lucid technical language. Although a flight might last only half an hour, the report might take several hours to write—and it had better be a good one if you wanted to complete No. 13 Course.

Kinch's principal instructors were Squadron Leader Ival "Tich" Crozier, a little R.A.F. veteran, and Wing Commander "Pop" Sewell, a big, bald, humorless Yorkshireman who talked without seeming to move his thin lips. They gave him his flying assignments and studied his reports.

Kinch and the other Americans were continually amazed at the "check-out" procedure for learning to fly the British airplanes they had never seen before. Go check out in the Vampire, they would be told, and they would go find the airplane, climb in the cockpit, study the Vampire handbook for a while, locate the various instruments and controls which are common to all aircraft, then take it off the ground, all without benefit of an instructor. It was a calculated if somewhat risky procedure, designed to breed confidence on the "do-it-yourself" theory.

Kinch soon checked out in all the planes at the E.T.P.S. and within the first few weeks of the course became recognized as one of the better pilots in the student group, although in academics he had to struggle to stay in the top half of the class. He was not concerned. It was not that he was neglecting his studies. Quite the opposite: he was studying harder than ever, but he had been thrown in with a group of the most brilliant pilots in the world.

Flying and academics were only two of the three areas on which the tutors graded their pupils. The third was "aptitude"—the "what-it-takes" in courage and character and ability to convey flight data to others to be a good test pilot. Kinch rated number one in that department.

In off-duty hours, he liked to go pub-crawling around the area or attend the point-to-point horse races. The ancient London cab, on which he had painted signs such as CAUTION: EJECTION SEAT, ONLY QUALIFIED OPERATORS MAY HANDLE, EMERGENCY EXIT, and HOT EXHAUST, became a familiar sight in the area around Farnborough. Loaded to more than capacity with student test pilots, "Lizzie" would cruise the area while Kinch, wearing a Sherlock Holmes hat he had picked up for "atmosphere," a cigar clenched in his teeth, would honk furiously on the rubber squeeze horn, drawing heavy-browed stares from the local bobbies.

On one occasion, Kinch, Dick Fernbaugh, Harry Julian, and the Italian Pete Trevisan made a trip to the Grand Prix race at Silverstone, a couple of hundred miles from Farnborough. They arrived early in the morning, to get a choice parking position near the finish line. It rained incessantly all that day and they were surrounded by a sea of English cars with steamed-up windows. "Lizzie" and its occupants drew more attention than the race; the cab itself was enough to attract interest, but Kinch and his partners had erected a huge canvas canopy on its roof. Underneath it, the four reclined in lawn chairs which Fernbaugh had brought over from the States, drinking cans of beer they had bought at the commissary and frying bacon and eggs on a primus stove. Despite the rain, the drenched passers-by would stop and survey the scene in amused wonderment.

During this period, Kinch developed an interest in art and music. From a Polish painter whom he had met through Bill Botts's wife he took art lessons, and with Harry Julian he would frequently make the one-hour run to London's Festival Hall, where he would listen entranced to the music of Bach and Beethoven, his favorite composers.

In early summer, he bought another British car, this time not an inexpensive relic, but a fine vintage racing auto, a 1924 Vauxhall 30/98 which he purchased for slightly over three hundred pounds from a collector in Farnham. He spent a lot of his time and money tuning it up, tightening the bolts, and repairing the furnishings. He planned to race it someday, and it was in the Vauxhall that he made one of his most dangerous "flights"—he test-drove the car to a speed of 119 miles per hour over the winding, narrow British roads.

In the mess at the E.T.P.S., Kinch became the acknowledged leader of the "prankster set." His favorite sport was ribbing Mr. Morley. He would hide a pair of shoes or a uniform, and stand by chuckling while the batman scurried nervously all over the building wondering how he could possibly have misplaced the gear. One night, caught up in the gaiety of a dinner party, he led a "revolt" that might have ended his test-pilot career. With assistance from two other student pilots, he grabbed "Sammie" Wroath, rolled the group captain neatly in a rug, and propped the rug upright in a corner of the dining room, occasionally pouring beer down the tube to "cool off" the howling commandant. Wroath, fortunately, had a sense of humor; he chalked it up to the high spirits he liked in a test pilot and good-naturedly laughed it off.

As part of his course in instruction, Kinch toured all the plants of the British aircraft industry, flying their newer planes and also their collection of vintage models, some of them older than his Vauxhall. It was good experience, he felt; he still wanted to learn all there was to know about flying, and the older planes taught him things he could not learn in the speedy jets.

In the course of his test-flying and some extracurricular flights, Kinch acquired a new distinction at the E.T.P.S. He became, as his messmates termed it, a "peacetime ace" by adding five British aircraft to the ten planes he had destroyed in Korea. Once, trying to spot-land a glider, he hit a cement retaining wall and tore off the tail. Again, he landed short in a Vampire and bounced off an embankment. On a third occasion, he accidentally taxied a Sea Fury into a drainage ditch. The fourth incident occurred when he volunteered to fly to the West of England to pick up the commandant's golf clubs, which Wroath had left there after a tournament. He arrived at dusk at a strange private field and overlooked a hump in its center, which drove his landing gear through the wings. His final "kill" came on a test flight when a helicopter started oscillating, went out of control, and crashed into the ground from low altitude.

Kinch was not hurt on any of the accidents and his instructors decided that the variety of circumstances indicated no loss of competence, so the five accidents did not affect his flying career. He incurred, however, severe ego damage from the ribbing he took in the mess.

At the halfway mark of No. 13 Course, the student pilots were given a summer break, a two-week vacation. Kinch, by now the most popular member of the mess, received a number of invitations from his colleagues to spend the fortnight with them. One, in particular, appealed to him because it was a chance to learn something new—yacht-sailing. Tony Blackman and a number of his R.A.F. friends had lined up a big yacht at Kiel in Germany, with which they planned a tour of the Baltic.

Blackman and Kinch loaded their gear into "Lizzie" and took off for Harwich, the embarkation port for Denmark. There they had "Lizzie" craned aboard the ship, to the accompaniment of laughs and cheers from customs officials, passengers, and crew. They unloaded the old cab at Esbjerg, Denmark, the following day and drove it to Kiel, where the Germans gave "Lizzie" the same wondering inspection it always occasioned in England.

For the next two weeks, in perfect weather, they cruised among the Danish islands and visited a number of harbors in Denmark, Norway, and Sweden, aboard the one-hundred-square-meter yacht the *Kronich*. Because of his lack of sailing experience, Kinch was at first assigned as crew tea-maker, a distasteful job to a tea-hater but one at which, characteristically, he worked to become expert; he learned it so well that even he began to drink tea. At the end of a week, he had picked up sailing techniques to the point that, if he was not a master, he was at least a valuable crew member. He was sorry when they cruised back into Kiel at the end of the fortnight; it had been a wonderful, relaxing vacation, a complete and exciting change from the rigorous grind at the E.T.P.S.

As "Lizzie" tooled back toward Farnborough, though, Kinch was seized with a new eagerness to get back in the cockpit. The old, passionate love for flying was still there; nothing could ever replace it.

IX. KINCH MEETS HIS FUTURE WIFE

$\mathbb{B}$ACK IN the United States, there were developments under way which had considerable effect on the life of Iven Kincheloe.

In Oakland, California, a slim, attractive, brunette receptionist for Kaiser Engineers named Dorothy Heinig was planning a trip to Europe. She had lined up three other girls. Joan Hale was a secretary at the Kaiser plant, Marilyn Gutierrez worked for *Sunset* magazine, and Marlene Dunn managed a French restaurant in Oakland. The girls had saved their money for months and now, with fifteen hundred dollars each, they were about to embark on a grand three-month tour of the Continent by auto, having bought a little Renault with a luggage rack for delivery in Paris.

The first leg of the journey was cross-country to New York, where they would board a liner. In New York, Dorothy was joined by Dolphin D. Overton III, Kinch's old jet-pilot buddy who had made good his boast to become a fighter ace after a tour in fighter-bombers. Dolph had met Dorothy on his return to the United States after his Korean tour, and while they were not engaged, it was a not remote possibility. He had taken a brief vacation from his lumber business in South Carolina to see Dorothy off.

"Look," he said, the night before she was to board the ship, "I have a very good friend who is at test-pilot school near London. He's a big, blond handsome guy and you'll like him. Look him up when you get there. His name is Iven Kincheloe."

Dorothy was not very interested; she didn't even like the name. Anyway, the girls had allotted only three days for London and she didn't think she would have much time for looking people up. She did not even bother to write down the odd name in the book of European contacts she had collected over the months.

The next day, the four girls boarded the *Ryndam*, a ship of the Holland-America Line, and sailed for seven days to Southampton, England. They took the boat train to Waterloo Station in London and there, in the confusion of the big city, without even a hotel reservation, they became slightly bewildered. They decided to call some of their contacts for help.

They became increasingly nervous as they failed to locate one after another of the contacts until they had exhausted the list. Then Dorothy remembered Dolph's friend with the odd name. Knowing only that he was in a test-pilot school, she miraculously located him with the help of a friendly phone operator.

Kinch was delighted to help any friend of old "D. D." He said he would arrange reservations at the Cumberland Hotel, a "nice, inexpensive place" which, the girls later found, was the most costly hotel they visited in all of Europe. He also volunteered to come in and show them the town, and Dorothy accepted, a trifle reluctantly but mindful now of the need for guidance in the big, strange city.

Kinch steamed up in "Lizzie" about an hour after the girls had settled in the hotel, bringing along Pete Trevisan and a brief case which bulged with a liquor bottle. For Dorothy, it was hardly "love at first sight." The big, husky blond was handsome in a way, she decided, but she was not impressed by his glib, fast-talking manner or the crazily decorated London cab. Kinch, though, knew from the start that flying had a competitor for his affections. He drank in his first view of the pretty, beautifully proportioned girl from Oakland and said to himself, "This is the one."

The four girls and the two pilots "did the town" that night, Kinch becoming more and more attracted to Dorothy, she entering into the spirit of his merry patter and finding that there was more to the big flyboy than her first impression had indicated. A romance was in bud. When Kinch returned to the mess that night, he barged into Tony Blackman's room and announced he had found the girl he was going to marry.

Kinch had no flying duty that weekend, so the next two days were one big whirl. They toured the sights of London, the Bridge and Tower, Windsor Castle, Buckingham Palace, and the Ascot race track. In the evenings, he brought all four girls out to the mess and pressed Trevisan, Julian, and Blackman into escort service. He "invited" the whole group to dinner parties at the off-base homes of Dick Fernbaugh and Bill Botts.

Then Dorothy's London stay was up and she hated to leave. Her first impression of Kinch had given way to a growing interest. She was still not sure she was in love, but certainly Iven Kincheloe was the most interesting man she had ever met. When Kinch drove her to the airport, he promised he would catch up with her somewhere on her tour of Europe, and she found herself hoping that he would.

Dorothy and her three companions picked up their Renault in Paris and started the Grand Tour. They drove to Lille, then to Brussels and Amsterdam and on into Germany. In Frankfurt, only a week after he had put her on the airplane, Kinch made good his promise to rejoin her. He flew over for the weekend, took all four girls to the American Club, and hustled dates for the others so he could be alone with Dorothy. That night, though he did not propose, he spent a lot of time explaining life in the Air Force, emphasizing the fact that he had worked all his twenty-six years to become a test pilot and he had no intention of abandoning the career for marriage. There was room in his heart for two loves, but he could not give up one for the other.

Kinch returned to Farnborough, after extracting a promise that Dorothy would come back to England at the end of her tour, and the girls resumed their travels. They went to Heidelberg and Salzburg, then to Vienna, where they stayed in the Soviet zone because it was the cheapest place they could find; on to Innsbruck, Zurich, Milan, Venice, Rome, Capri, Nice, Cannes and, in November, 1954, to Barcelona and Madrid, the last leg of the scheduled tour.

Meanwhile, Kinch had entered the final phase of No. 13 Course. Although four of his classmates had "washed out," he was no longer worried about completing the course. Inspired by the new thought of marriage to Dorothy, he had worked harder than ever on the difficult academic portion of his work and had pulled his grades up a few notches. He was flying better than ever and the test reports he turned in were sharp and concise but thorough. On aptitude he had the highest possible rating.

No. 13 Course was in its final fortnight when Dorothy returned to England. He persuaded her to stay on until his graduation, and because she had practically exhausted her long-saved money, arranged for her to live the last two weeks with the Fernbaughs. Dick and Mike Fernbaugh lived close to the base and Kinch was able to see Dorothy every day. They visited all his favorite pubs, frequented the "cinema," and took walking tours around the countryside.

It was time for Kinch to go back to the Air Force, and he had one big scare when he was told his new assignment would be back at Nellis Air Force Base, but the Pentagon apparently reconsidered and sent word of a new job: test pilot at Edwards Air Force Base, the long-awaited goal! Kinch's happiness was complete.

He was forced to part with "Lizzie." The colorful taxi had served him well, but he planned to ship the Vauxhall back to the United States and he could not afford to bring both cars. Sadly he sold "Lizzie" for four pounds more than he had paid for her.

And then came the Graduation Ball. It was a colorful affair in a gaily decorated ballroom, with a big orchestra, a champagne bar, and a regular bar. The officers wore dress uniforms with swords and the Queen sent her personal representative.

Between dances, Kinch took Dorothy outside and proposed. Neither of them remembered later just what he said, but it mattered little. Dorothy no longer had any doubts; if she had any qualms about marrying a test pilot, they were overcome by the knowledge she could marry no one else. She accepted, and they agreed to wait until their return to the States.

Kinch said his good-bys to the wonderful group he had lived with for ten months—"Sammie" Wroath, the commandant, and Mr. Morley, the worshipful batman, Dick Fernbaugh and Bill Botts, Harry Julian and Tony Blackman,

Pete Trevisan and "Bancho" and the others who had survived the course.

No. 13 Course had been a great experience and it had sharpened his skill as a pilot and broadened his knowledge of the aeronautical realm. Now there were still bigger things to come, as test pilot first class.

X. A NEW DREAM—THE X-2

I̶T WAS mid-January, 1955, when Kinch reported to the Air Force Flight Test Center at Edwards Air Force Base. The month since his graduation at Farnborough had been a hectic one. He and Dorothy had spent a few days on a last look at Paris, then, while she went to Washington to visit relatives, he flew back to Cassopolis to see his parents and pick up the black Cadillac he had left there.

He drove the Cadillac to Washington and spent New Year's Eve with Dorothy. Together they went to New York, where he bought an engagement ring and wedding band and picked up the Vauxhall racer which had followed him by ship. Towing the Vauxhall behind the Cadillac, they drove to Cassopolis, where Dorothy was presented to Kinch's parents. After an announcement party in Oakland, at which Kinch met Dorothy's family and friends, he drove alone to Edwards.

It was a thrill just to be stationed at Edwards, in whatever capacity. There was something exciting going on every hour of the day.

The Air Force Flight Test Center was one of several test-and-research centers within the Air Research and Development Command. Its mission was to test and evaluate the latest research and production aircraft of the U.S.A.F. and the Navy, and to conduct advanced research to be used in developing planes of still greater performance.

Edwards was a big, sprawling base, spreading out over some three hundred thousand acres of the Mojave Desert, about one hundred miles northeast of Los Angeles. It had an excellent climate for flight-testing: the desert was relatively free from storms and the Center operators could count on 350 days a year of good flying weather.

Heart of the base was the flight line, with its hangars housing the new planes. Adjacent to the flight line was one of the longest runways in the world, fifteen thousand feet of heavy concrete, wide as the length of a football field, where high-performing aircraft which landed at more than two hundred miles an hour could be tested safely. The runway ran right to the edge of Rogers Dry Lake, with its surface of fine clay and silt which had almost the same consistency as concrete, permitting use of the whole twelve-mile length of the lake bed as an emergency runway.

Flight-testing was not the only activity at Edwards. There was a variety of small units for testing the various components of an airplane; there was a missile-test section for evaluating high-thrust rocket engines; a parachute-test group; and a high-speed, 20,000-foot track on which rocket sleds crashed along at more than four times the speed of sound, testing various aircraft structures, ejection seats, and parachute deployment.

Flight-testing, though, was the major activity. In addition to the Air Force installation, the civilian government test agency, the National Advisory Committee for Aeronautics, maintained a separate research unit at one end of the base.

About forty aircraft and missile manufacturing companies had their own facilities at Edwards.

Testing a new airplane was a long, exacting, and time-consuming job. It was broken down into several phases. In Phase I, the manufacturing company's own test pilot would put the plane through an initial series of "airworthiness" tests, to demonstrate to the Air Force or Navy, the eventual user, that the plane could live up to the performance guarantees made for it.

Then, in Phase II, Air Force or Navy pilots would take over and give the same plane a more rigorous shakedown, noting deficiencies in design or performance and making recommendations as to how to correct them. In Phase III, the contractor would again take over the plane for a complete examination of the deficiencies noted. After they were corrected, the plane went back to the Air Force for Phase IV—a detailed check of its performance and stability.

A less glamorous but equally necessary test job at Edwards was Phase VI, or the functional-development test given a production airplane after all its original bugs had been ironed out. This was the type of job Iven Kincheloe had handled in his earlier brief assignment to Edwards. It consisted of flying a lot of hours in the airplane in a short time, to set up the handbooks for maintenance, inspection, and parts requirements. There were other test phases to which an airplane was subjected before it could be approved as "operational," such as all-weather capability and simulated combat tests, but these were conducted at other Air Force installations.

On the top rung of the test ladder was the most exciting and most dangerous job of all—advanced research work. This was performed in rocket-powered aircraft never designed for combat use: their job was solely to explore new areas of speed and altitude, regions which the combat aircraft could not penetrate, and bring data on which to base design of the next generation of aircraft.

There were three such planes flying when Kinch reported to Edwards. All built by Bell Aircraft and similar to each other, they were the Bell X-1A, X-1D, and X-1E. Their mighty rocket power plants gave them only a couple of minutes' powered-flight duration, but in that brief time the planes could accelerate to fantastic performances. In the X-1A, Major Charles "Chuck" Yeager had flown over 1,650 miles an hour, twice as fast as the most powerful operational jet being tested. Just a few months before Kinch reported to Edwards, Major Arthur "Kit" Murray had taken the same plane to a new altitude record of over 90,000 feet.

Even the incredible X-1A was soon to be dwarfed in performance capability. A manned missile named the X-2 was coming along. The previous year, the Flight Test Center had conducted a series of glide tests to check out the X-2's handling characteristics prior to attempting powered flight. It was now being reworked at Bell Aircraft's plant in Buffalo, New York, and was due back at the base in the summer. With a super-rocket power plant of far greater thrust than that of the X-1A, the X-2 had been designed to fly three times the speed of sound, more than 2,000 miles an hour, or climb as high as 135,000 feet, into the vacuum of inner space which was the next goal of flight researchers. The very thought of handling an airplane like that made Kinch's spirits soar.

But flying the hot rocket planes was not a job assigned to test pilots fresh from school. These tasks fell to the skilled senior pilots, men with years of test work behind them, men like Lieutenant Colonel Frank "Pete" Everest, who was considered the U.S.A.F.'s number-one test man, and Lieuten-

Photo, U.S. Air Force

Kincheloe and the X-2.

X-2 in powered flight, just after drop from B-50.

Photo, Bell Aircraft

Kincheloe (center) with his Purdue flying club, preparatory to leaflet-dropping expedition over the campus of rival Indiana University.

Kincheloe during summer encampment of Reserve Officers Training Corps at Wright-Patterson AFB, Dayton, Ohio.

Kincheloe as jet trainee, mounting T-33 trainer at Wiliiams AFB, Arizona.

7-1948
DAYTON
OHIO

Kincheloe receiving the Silver Star from General Frank Everest in Korea.

Kincheloe and the aircraft he flew.

Photo, Hal Matson

Kincheloe's wedding at Carmel Mission, California. *Top left:* In England
with Dorothy and the Tin Lizzie, near Windsor Castle.

Kincheloe with baby son "Sam."

After the christening.

Photo, U.S. Air Force

Kincheloe and the X-2.

Kincheloe receives the Mackay Trophy from General Thomas D. White,
Chief of Staff of the United States Air Force.

Kincheloe in X-15.

ant Colonel Jack Ridley, Edwards' chief of engineering, and N.A.C.A.'s civilian pilot, Scott Crossfield.

Rookies like Kinch had to start at the bottom rung. They were not even assigned the routine phase tests; instead, they had to break in as "chase" pilots. A chase pilot flew alongside a test airplane and watched for external troubles the test pilot might not be able to detect. This was a necessary if unspectacular job and it gave the new pilot a chance to get the "feel" of what was going on at Edwards.

Kinch's first assignment at Edwards was as a member of the Fighter Branch of the Flight Test Operations Division. His boss was Pete Everest, whom he had met and liked during his earlier visits to Edwards. Among his co-workers were his old friends from Korea and Nellis, Bill Westcott and Dave Freeland, and another friend, from his first Edwards stint, Major Stuart Childs, now a veteran test pilot. His first jobs were routine chases for contractor test pilots.

As soon as he was settled in the Edwards routine, Kinch formulated the Master Plan. He was happy in his lot, but he had not spent all the years of preparation to fly chase on a lumbering transport airplane. He had to get into the newer airplanes and, eventually, the advanced rocket jobs, maybe even the X-2. It was ambitious, but why not? Pete Everest was now doing most of the rocket work, and Pete had already served nearly nine years of test flying. Sooner or later, the Air Force would reassign Everest as a matter of policy, because the top brass recognized you couldn't buck the odds forever. Then they would look around for a replacement. There were a great many pilots at Edwards senior to Kinch in flying time and rank, but with characteristic confidence, he felt there were not too many who could outfly him. When the brass started looking around for a new rocket man, Kinch was going to be ready.

The first step, he decided, was to pile up more flying time. At Edwards, they were not too interested in a pilot's total flying time; he could, for instance, have thousands of hours in a transport plane, or even a fighter, and be totally unqualified as a test pilot. The consideration that counted was how many *test* hours the pilot had flown, and how aptly he had handled his assignments.

From Captain Lou Schalk, like himself a newcomer to the base, he learned the trick of getting extra assignments. When not flying, most of the pilots lolled about the lounge, reading or "swapping lies." Not Schalk. He usually hung close to the dispatcher's desk and when a call came in from a contractor requesting a chase pilot, he volunteered immediately and usually got the assignment on the basis of proximity.

Kinch started joining Schalk in the dispatcher's office and it worked. Within a few weeks, he was flying twice as many missions as his less eager co-workers, chase stuff to be sure, dull from the flying standpoint but sometimes interesting because he was chasing brand-new airplanes and learning about them.

His eagerness impressed Pete Everest, who had become a close friend of Kinch's, and Major Stephens, chief of the Fighter Branch. They gave him an assignment to a specific project, investigating a gunnery defect in the new, supersonic F-100, big brother of the F-86 he had flown in Korea. His role was a minor one—towing the air-to-air targets while Stephens, the project officer, poured round after round at them trying to learn what was wrong with the gun mounts.

It was a spear-carrying part, but at least he was in a program. It was a step.

"It's a low form of existence for a pilot of my potential greatness," he joked with Schalk, "but you watch, I'll be flying that airplane before the program is over."

He was. Before long, he had talked Stephens into letting

him take a few shots at the tow target, and with his natural ability and Korean War experience, he was better at the air-to-air gunnery than anyone who had tried the F-100. When a new model of the F-100 came in from the North American plant and Fighter Branch was instructed to run a similar program, Kinch got the nod, months before he had any right to expect a project assignment. The Master Plan was progressing.

Within the next few months, Kinch moved rapidly up the ladder. Pete Everest, who had watched him closely and was aware of his great natural aptitude for test work, brought him along fast. Kinch ran a number of routine Phase IV's and Phase VI's, then moved up to Phase-II tests on the new "100 series" of supersonic aircraft—the McDonnell F-101, the Convair F-102, the Republic F-105, and the Lockheed F-104. In these tests he was flying brand-new, "hot" aircraft, running the initial Air Force evaluations after the contractors had made only a few demonstration flights.

It was fascinating work, just what he had been after for years. It had the thrill and adventure which he had sought since his earliest flying days and he reveled in every moment of it. But he had fixed his eye on a still more distant goal.

The fabulous X-2 had arrived at Edwards. Kinch got a look at it as it sat in its hangar, sleek and powerful in appearance. It had a long fuselage made of K-monel metal and its wing and tail surfaces were of stainless steel to resist the terrific temperatures it would encounter as it smashed through the air mass at speeds of more than 2,000 miles per hour. Its mighty, throttleable rocket engine, consisting of a large tube and a smaller one, could blast out 15,000 pounds of thrust. It was so fast it had no ordinary ejection seat, since the wind blast in a high-speed ejection would be severe enough to kill the pilot; the X-2 had a system wherein the whole cockpit could be blasted away from the fuselage and lowered by parachute. Like all the previous rocket planes, with their limited power duration, it was designed to be carried aloft by a mother plane and dropped at altitude. Hence, it had no main wheels for take-off; it had the normal nose wheel and a pair of retractable skids for landing on the clay surface of Rogers Dry Lake.

From the moment Kinch saw the X-2, he knew his career would never be complete until he had flown it. It was unlikely that he would. Everest had been assigned the initial test program and when he had completed a series of flights, the X-2 was to be turned over to the National Advisory Committee for Aeronautics, for further testing. Nonetheless, Kinch decided to become a rocket expert—just in case.

The Kincheloe Master Plan turned toward rocketry. He had learned something about rocket-powered aircraft at the Empire Test Pilots' School, but he hardly qualified as an expert.

He started out by reading every volume he could find on the workings of rocket engines. He read the flight reports of all the rocket-powered flights ever made at Edwards, from Chuck Yeager's first supersonic runs in 1947 to the latter-day work of Everest and Ridley in the X-1A and Everest's previous year's glide flights in the X-2.

Then he began his customary brain-picking operation. He haunted the rocket area, quizzing everyone from the top scientists and engineers in the program down to the lowliest technician in charge of tightening nuts and bolts, taking a daily brain transfusion, trying to absorb the world's accumulated rocket lore.

Meanwhile, when they were not answering Kinch's questions, the members of the X-2 project group were readying the plane for its first flight, running a series of ground checks on the rocket engine and the various systems in the airplane. It was a painstaking process of check and double check, but with a plane of the X-2's performance capability, nothing could be left to chance.

In early August, the extensive ground checks uncovered a source of trouble—defective gaskets in the power-plant system. The first powered flight was postponed indefinitely.

By this time, Kinch had another great adventure in process. Throughout his first six months at Edwards, he had commuted on week ends to Oakland to see Dorothy. Now they had set the date for the wedding and even the X-2 had to take a back seat. For the first time in the twenty-seven years of his existence, Iven Kincheloe had encountered something more important than flying.

XI. KINCH TAKES OVER AS ROCKET PILOT NUMBER ONE

THE WEDDING of Dorothy Heinig and Iven Carl Kincheloe, Jr., took place on August 20, 1955, at the beautiful and historic Carmel Mission in Carmel, California. The wedding party was a mixture of Air Force people from Edwards, Dorothy's relatives and friends from the Oakland–San Francisco area, and the Kincheloe family from Cassopolis. As might be expected, the man who had ice water in his veins when it came to flying the fastest and trickiest airplanes built was a nervous bridegroom.

There was a reception after the ceremony at Highlands Inn, near the Mission, then the wedding party broke up bit by bit and Kinch was alone with his wife. They stayed at Carmel for a week, moved to the Mark Hopkins Hotel in San Francisco for a few more days, and finally drove back to Edwards early in September to take up their life together at the test base.

Quarters were hard to come by on the crowded base, but Kinch had managed to get a sublease on a home from an officer who was on extended temporary duty at another base.

By the time the occupant returned, Kinch was assured, he would have his own house.

Their new home was a two-bedroom place in the Wherry housing area, a few miles from the center of the base, where there were row upon row of small homes monotonously similar to each other. It was not luxurious, but it was adequate. Kinch was ecstatically happy and for all he cared, they could have lived in a hangar.

It was not Dorothy's first view of the base. Earlier in the year she had come down to Edwards for a four-day visit, and that visit had done little to ease her mind about marriage to a test pilot. At a cocktail party the night of her arrival, she had met a number of Kinch's fellow officers. One of them was Captain Paul Bryce, a member of the Fighter Branch. The following day, Bryce was killed on a Phase II mission.

Life in the Wherry area was not always tense. The test pilots were few in number compared with the large roster of civilians, airmen, and officers who staffed the base, and the test pilots' wives for the most part were calm about their husbands' occupations. Still, there was always that awful moment when the pall of blue smoke rose from the desert, the sirens sounded, and the crash trucks went screaming toward the accident. Who was the pilot and had he got out before the crash? Most of the time, the smoke signified only an airplane burning while the pilot floated to safety in a parachute, but fatalities were frequent enough. Even the names of the streets in the housing area—Gregorius, Forbes, Wolfe, Bailey, Seller, Popson, Payne, Fitzgerald—were constant reminders of the hazards of test-flying, for they were named for pilots who had been killed while engaged in test work. And the base itself, of course, was similarly named.

Dorothy Kincheloe was determined to be one of the calm wives. It served no purpose to worry constantly, and, anyway,

Dorothy shared Kinch's own philosophy about accidents: they were bound to happen, but he had spent years preparing for emergencies and felt that when something went wrong, he had the skill to handle it. There was, however, always the possibility of the type of accident which no amount of skill could forestall—the swift visitation of death, which was ever present on a test flight of a new, untried plane. Dorothy thrust that possibility to the back of her mind.

Kinch took to home life easily. He gave up his nightly visit to the Officers' Club for a hangar-talk session and came straight home from the flight line each evening. He liked to change to a pair of shapeless slacks and a T shirt and loll about the house, listening to his favorite Mantovani-style dreamy music, which had supplanted Bach and Beethoven. He loved to entertain, and with his flair for storytelling and his big, booming, ready laugh, he was always the life of the party. He had a constant stream of visitors coming to the house, because he was proud of Dorothy's beauty and wanted everybody on the base to meet her. To each of them he made a standard introduction: "This is my lovely wife, Dorothy."

Dorothy met a lot of Kinch's friends and bosses during those first few weeks at Edwards. There was the Center commander, Brigadier General J. Stanley Holtoner, and his Director of Flight Test, Colonel Horace Hanes, and, of course, Pete Everest and Stu Childs, whom she had met before. There were a number of new friends, either from Kinch's Fighter Branch or other sections of the Test Center, like Lou Schalk, Pat Hunerwadel, Jim Carson, Bob Hippert, Joe Jordan, Bob White, Mel Apt, and Bob Titus, several of whom later joined the ranks of the great test pilots of the Air Force. Dorothy got along fine with most of the wives, and became close friends with some of them.

Kinch was flying again, but during the first couple of

months after his marriage it was largely routine. He was guilty of one small "goof" that might have been serious. One day, when he was scheduled to chase, the test plane took off ahead of schedule and Kinch charged out of operations, late. In his haste to get airborne, he made only the quickest of inspections of his chase plane, overlooking the bright-red plug in the nose of the engine which guarded against engine damage on the ground.

He started up the engine and the powerful suction "inhaled" the plug into the intake, where it stuck, partially blocking the air flow. This substantially reduced his available power, but Kinch didn't notice it until he was rolling down the runway at high speed. It was too late to shut down and stop. He managed to lift the underpowered plane off the runway, stagger around the field, and land, aborting his mission.

Kinch might have alibied his way out of the error by blaming the crew chief, but, typically, he took the whole responsibility and made a gag out of it. He went straight to the operations lounge and told the story to everyone there, with embellishments and hand gestures.

"It's a good thing it was Kincheloe, though, and no one else," he concluded in mock-seriousness. "A lesser pilot just couldn't have handled it." His bosses liked the way he shouldered the blame and the goof became an asset rather than a setback.

He was still hard at the Master Plan to get himself a part in the X-2 program, reading and quizzing incessantly. Now the Plan took a new turn. He had learned a great deal about rocket power and decided it was time to let someone know it; actually, he knew more about the rocket planes than anyone on the base except those already intimately connected with the X-2. You couldn't just walk up to someone, though, and say, "I'm a rocket expert." Kinch adopted a more subtle approach.

It was the custom on the base for the manufacturers to present models of the various airplanes to the Air Force pilots who tested them. These models were prized possessions, and the most prized of all was an X-1 model, because so few pilots had flown the plane. Kinch had no claim to one, of course, but he determined to get one anyway, by a roundabout method.

With scrap metal from an X-1 that had crashed, he fashioned his own model of the plane, a crude and horrible-looking thing, and plumped it on the middle of his desk. He called it the Fish Hook and waited for it to catch something. One day, a Bell Aircraft representative happened into the office and took the bait. Questioned about the Hook, Kinch explained that he had not, of course, ever flown the X-1, but that he had been terribly interested in the program and had built the model out of sentiment, for after all, the crude model was fashioned from parts of the fastest plane on earth. The Bell man did not notice the twinkle in Kinch's eye. Impressed by Kinch's interest in the X-1, or perhaps eager to get the monstrous Hook out of circulation, he presented Kinch with a model of the X-1.

This gave Kinch the opening he was looking for. Visitors to the office he shared with Lou Schalk would immediately notice the X-1 sitting proudly on Kinch's desk and ask if he had flown it.

"No," Kinch would start slowly, "I never had the opportunity, but I've always wished I could have flown it, because—" and then he would be off on a rapid-fire dissertation on what he would have tried to do with the airplane and what he could have learned. Because Kinch *did* know what he was talking about, his little lecture never failed to impress.

The ruse worked; his knowledge of rocketry was brought to the attention of the proper people.

As another part of his Master Plan, Kinch had taken to "joining." He joined all the aeronautical societies and some others—the Institute of Aeronautical Sciences, the American Rocket Society, the Aircraft Owners and Pilots Association, the American Society of Mechanical Engineers, the Air Force Association, the American Institute of Management, and, later, when it was formed, the Society of Experimental Test Pilots.

One day, Lou Schalk asked Kinch how come all this interest in joining things. Kinch had to pay dues to all of them, and the return on the investment seemed slim to Schalk.

"Maybe so, Lou," Kinch replied, "but there are an awful lot of smart guys in those societies, and I feel that some of it is bound to rub off. Besides, it just plain looks good—it's like having a bunch of degrees."

In his off-duty hours at Edwards, Kinch took up a new venture—theatrical producing. It was the custom at the Test Center to throw a going-away party for every departing officer, and transfers were frequent. The highlight of each of these parties was a traditional skit, in which the departing officer would be lampooned by his fellows. It took a nice, light, satiric touch to do it properly, but Kinch had that kind of sense of humor. When the regular scripter-producer team left the base, Kinch volunteered for the job and formed the team of Schalk and Kincheloe, writers-producers-actors. They were extremely good at it, and the old-timers at Edwards still remember the blackface act Kinch and Pat Hunerwadel put on for these shows; it was hilarious, and everybody said, "It should be on Broadway."

Since before Kinch's wedding, the X-2 project group had been hard at work readying the X-2 for its first powered flight. Late in October, the final ground run was made, the plane approved, and the flight scheduled for mid-November. Kinch "sweated it out" while the Center bosses debated the make-up of the flying cast. Everest would fly the X-2, of course, but there were a number of other assignments, such as chase and photographic planes. He went into raptures when he got the word: he would fly one of the two chase planes.

On November 17, a B-50 hauled the X-2 to drop altitude, Kinch flying chase, but broken cloud cover made the weather marginal. Everest was as eager as anyone to try the powered run, but he was also an old hand at flight-testing, and there was a saying that "There are old pilots and bold pilots, but no old bold pilots." Common sense prevailed and Everest canceled the drop.

The next day the weather was fine. The formation of the B-50 with its precious cargo, the X-2, the photo planes, and the chase planes swept over the dry lake and suddenly the X-2 was dropping on its own. For this flight, Everest was to use only the smaller, 5,000-pound-thrust rocket chamber; it ignited in a sheet of flame. The rocket plane roared upward, away from the formation. It climbed to 45,000 feet, reaching a speed just under that of sound, and then the rocket engine burned out prematurely and quit. Everest jettisoned the remaining fuel and started a spiral glide down to the lake bed.

As he dropped his skids and nose wheel for the landing, Kinch noticed the nose wheel was cocked at a forty-five-degree angle. He reported it immediately to Everest. It was a potentially dangerous situation, but Everest was not excited; he never was. If the nose wheel straightened out, it would be all right; if it did not, there was danger of a ground loop, which could result in minor scraping of a wing tip or wrapping the whole plane up into a ball.

Everest, allowing himself plenty of room for the anticipated ground loop, brought the rocket plane in nicely and touched down at two hundred miles an hour; the nose wheel thumped once at its cocked angle, then straightened out.

It seemed like a reasonably successful first flight, but the post-mission detailed examination brought bad news. One of the landing skids had been damaged. In addition, investigation of the premature shutdown disclosed evidence of a fire in the engine compartment, and the inspecting team was not satisfied with the way the fuel-jettisoning system had worked. The plane would have to go back to the plant for extensive re-work and the program would be delayed for months.

Kinch went back to less spectacular flying, but he was given an assignment that held a great deal of interest for him. North American Aviation had come up with a new model of the F-100 called the F-100C. Kinch was named project officer to run the Phase IV stability-and-control tests and, concurrently, the Phase VI functional-development test. During the winter of 1955 and into the spring of 1956, he flew more than one hundred flights on this new plane, checking its handling characteristics in all types of configurations, with external fuel tanks and with bombs and rockets mounted under the wings and fuselage. Part of the program called for a series of L.A.B.S. (Low Altitude Bombing System) tests, using a dummy nuclear bomb, in which Kinch would scream in at low altitude, pull up in a sharp climb, release the "A bomb" at a preselected point, then pour on the afterburner, the auxiliary power system, for a fast dash to altitude to get out of the way of the "nuclear explosion." It was interesting flying and the F-100C turned out to be a good plane—in Kinch's report, "a formidable ground-support weapon." It took his mind off the X-2, but he never really forgot the wonderful rocket plane.

The X-2 was back at the base at the end of February, 1956,

and the interminable series of ground runs and checks started. Again, it appeared to be ready and a flight was conducted on March 24, this time using the 10,000-pound chamber. The big chamber worked all right, but when Everest tried to cut in the smaller, 5,000-pound rocket, it failed to ignite. He made several tries, but no go. There was another month's delay while the engineers devised a new starter circuit.

On April 25, Everest finally achieved supersonic flight with the X-2, but the 10,000-pound rocket chamber worked sporadically and he was not able to push it to high performance. Even so, he climbed to 50,000 feet and reached a speed of Mach 1.4, one and four-tenths the speed of sound or about 925 miles per hour. It was the best flight yet and there was general jubilance among the project group; it looked as though the major bugs had been ironed out and they could soon "go for the moon."

After relocation of a fuel line to take care of the trouble with the big chamber, Everest went again on May 1, with Kinch flying low chase. Kinch's major job in this position was to check the control movements of the X-2 prior to drop while Everest manipulated the stick, because Pete, his cockpit nestled inside the bomb bay of the B-50, could not see the control surfaces.

The controls worked perfectly and the X-2 was dropped at 30,000 feet. Everest started the small rocket tube; it lighted normally and the X-2 started to climb. Everest ignited the larger chamber, and Kinch, flying behind him, immediately reported a fire in "big ten." Everest shut down the larger chamber and the fire was extinguished; he tried another start. This time it was all right. The X-2 roared away from Kinch in a steep climb. Pete took it up to fifty thousand feet, both chambers working well, and pushed it over into a slight dive to pick up momentum. Before the engines cut out, Everest attained a speed of Mach 1.68, slightly more than 1,100 miles an hour.

The rocket program was in high gear now. It took only eleven days to get the X-2 back in the air again. On this, the fifth powered flight, Everest and the X-2 moved still faster and higher, climbing to 60,000 feet, then picking up speed in a flat dive, rocketing to Mach 1.8, or more than 1,200 miles per hour.

The plane was right now; the project group felt it was time to "expand the envelope," to push the X-2 up to the greater speeds and altitudes of which it was theoretically capable.

And then came the terrific news that Kinch had been waiting for. Pete Everest had been alerted by the high command that he would be transferred to a new operational assignment in Germany on or about July 1. There were still at least five flights to go to complete the envelope of the X-2's performance, possibly more if something went wrong on any one of the flights. Everest might not have time to make all of them. General Holtoner, the Center commander, decided it was time to find an alternate pilot for Everest, to check him out and have him in reserve in case Pete could not complete the program.

As soon as the grapevine circulated the news, Kinch hastened to volunteer. He not only volunteered to Everest and Hanes, the Director of Flight Test, he volunteered to everyone who listened. He pointed out his intensive research into rocket power, his familiarity with the program as chase pilot, and anything else he could think of that might be a contributing factor. He had to fly that airplane!

He was not the only volunteer; every qualified pilot at the Center wanted the X-2, or even a single flight in it.

There was a tense period while the Center bosses mulled it over. They called in Everest, who as immediate chief of the

99

test pilots best knew his crew, and asked for his recommendations. Everest, who had been anticipating a transfer for some time, had given it a lot of thought. He named Iven Kincheloe as primary alternate, little, balding Mel Apt, Kinch's friend from Fighter Branch, as secondary.

There was one problem, Holtoner and Hanes pointed out. The cockpit of the X-2, tiny to begin with and crammed with instrumentation, left little room for a man. Everest, though stocky and muscular, was only five feet eight inches tall. Could Kincheloe, who topped him by five and a half inches and had broader shoulders, squeeze into the cockpit and still handle the controls? Everest didn't know; that was why he had named Apt as secondary.

The next morning, Everest took Kinch and Mel Apt over to the Bell Aircraft hangar to meet Bob Lapp, Bell's project director, and Jimmy Powell, the company's flight-test engineer. He introduced them as his understudies.

Lapp and Powell looked dubiously at Kincheloe. Kinch read their minds.

"Sure I can fit into the cockpit," he blurted out. "I'll slouch down a little bit and have my parachute repacked so it will be flat and I'll wear my dress shoes which are much smaller than the ones I have on. I'll fit, all right—I just won't rattle around as much as the others."

Powell took the two pilots over to the plane and gestured to Kinch; there was no need to worry about Apt, because he was smaller than Everest. Kinch climbed up on the wing and lowered himself into the seat.

"Just a little snug." He grinned weakly. The group of onlookers said nothing. Everyone knew how badly he wanted this airplane, but they could see that wearing only his summer khakis, he filled the cockpit to absolute capacity. For flight he would have to wear the bulky pressure suit.

Powell called the Bell equipment man, who stepped up on the wing and measured clearances. He stepped down, shaking his head.

"We'll have to shrink him if he's going to fly this plane," he said.

Kinch leaped out of the cockpit, his ears flaming.

"O.K., then. By damn, I'll shrink myself," he shouted. "I'm going to fly this plane!" He grabbed Jimmy Powell by the arm. "Let's get out of here so we can talk this thing over."

They went over to the Service Club for a cup of coffee. Methodically, like a lawyer presenting a case, Kinch unfolded his story. He had been pointing for something like this all his life. The X-2 was a space plane, one which could go as high as the start of the vacuum. Behind it, in a few years, would come planes of even greater performance; that was inevitable. They would go still farther into space. In short, the man who replaced Everest now would be the first of the spacemen. That had been Kinch's goal for a long time; he was not going to be stopped now by a couple of inches of cockpit clearance. He alternately pounded and pleaded, and Jimmy Powell was impressed by the intensity of his desire.

"Slow down, boy," he said. "I'm convinced, but there still is only so much space available and you'll have to be able to get full throw on the controls and be able to reach all the switches. Then we'll have to convince the powers that be that you can do it. Bring over your pressure suit this afternoon and we'll give it a try."

That afternoon, Kinch reported with his pressure suit. The Bell crew was planning a ground check of the power-control system, and to fit Kinch into the schedule, he would have to sit in the cockpit with the engine running. On the ground this was plain murder; in the cramped cockpit even a much smaller man would feel as though he were in the world's hottest steam bath. With Kinch dressed in the pressure suit, it would be a tougher workout than any he ever had had.

They pressed him into the seat and it took two men to clamp down the canopy, forcing his head down into the cockpit so that he had to sit hunched over and look up to see the instrument panel. The control-system run was started and the cockpit got hot, then unpleasant, then downright torturous. But, to the onlookers watching and listening on the intercom, expecting a plea for release from the cockpit furnace, there was never a peep from Kinch. They all watched in admiration as the seconds ticked off. Just toward the end of the run, Kinch's voice came weakly over the intercom, not begging for a shutdown, just trying to make a gag of it.

"Hey, you guys, I'm nearly drowned in my own juice. The cockpit is nearly half full."

The power-system check was completed and Kinch crawled out, as wet as if he had been swimming. He was pale but grinning. "Told you," he croaked.

The Bell men who had been calling him Captain started calling him Kinch right then, and although they hated the very thought of any change that might interfere with the program, one of the engineers cleared his throat and suggested mildly that perhaps they could modify the cockpit to give him a little extra room, and another chimed in with a suggestion as to how. Everyone wanted to buy Kinch a Coke. Bob Lapp smiled; Kinch had made up their minds for them. He had "shrunk himself" with a display of guts that convinced every member of the crew that this was the guy they wanted in their airplane.

With the aid of the Bell crew and Pete Everest, Kinch convinced the Center bosses that he could fit in the X-2 cockpit. It would never be completely comfortable, but he could handle all the controls. He was officially named Everest's alternate, with the understanding that Everest would continue to fly until he had to leave the base.

It was decided to go ahead and expand the envelope of X-2 performance. The immediate goals were a speed of Mach 3 and an altitude of 100,000 feet, although theoretically the plane could do better than that.

Everest flew again on May 22, with Kinch riding as primary chase pilot. This time Pete pushed the top speed well over the Mach 2 mark. With both thrust tubes working normally, he climbed to 60,000 feet after the drop, pushed over into the dive, and at 57,000 feet the Mach needle climbed to 2.47, close to 1,650 miles per hour. It was the fastest speed ever recorded in an airplane. Everest reported some buffeting and a minor pitching oscillation, which was controllable. Other than that, the flight had been perfect.

Three days later, Kinch was given his first check ride in the X-2, with Everest flying in Kinch's old familiar chase spot. The results came nowhere near Everest's record-breaking achievement, but to Kinch, just handling the controls as the X-2 dropped out of its carrier's bomb bay made it successful.

He jockeyed the X-2 into the proper climb angle after he had started power, and at 41,000 feet he leveled off slightly to pick up speed. The needle topped Mach 1, then he started the climb again. And then the 10,000-pound-thrust chamber quit with a rumble. He made several tries to restart it, but nothing availed. As he dropped down again to 40,000 feet, he decided the engine was dead for this flight, jettisoned the remaining fuel, turned toward the dry lake and spiraled down to a perfect landing.

For a first check flight, it was a good one. Although he had accomplished nothing toward increasing the performance of the X-2, he had handled the airplane well throughout the flight and satisfied the center chiefs that he would be able to carry on when Everest left. He had flown the X-2, that was the big thing, and control-wise it had handled perfectly. In his post-flight report, Kinch wrote:

"Without a doubt, it was the greatest flight of my life."

After Kinch's check-out, the plane went back to the hangar for modification, to prepare it for a series of "maximum-effort" runs, reaching for 100,000 feet and Mach 3. Everest's departure was delayed for a month so he would be able to "go for broke" on speed.

Everest made a good try on July 12, but this time he had trouble controlling the plane and he also experienced another premature shutdown of the balky, complex power system. He did get up to 67,000 feet and Mach 1.5 before he had to turn for the lake.

Pete's departure for Europe was now imminent. He had time for one more flight and on July 23 he made it. This time it was near-perfect. Immediately after the drop, Pete hit both thrust chambers simultaneously and the X-2 spurted away from Kinch in the chase plane in a matter of seconds.

Because of the high acceleration, Everest had trouble holding the plane in the predetermined climb angle for maximum speed. He held it close enough, however, and the plane shot through the sky at a tremendous rate in a climb angle slightly higher than planned. At 50,000 feet, Everest gently nosed it forward, and at 65,000, leveled it off. In level flight, the plane shot ahead still faster, theMach needle climbing: 2.5, already above the previous record, 2.6, 2.7, 2.8, 2.85, and finally, as the rocket engines ate up the last of their fuel, 2.87, almost 1,900 miles an hour, just a hair's breadth on the Machmeter from the goal of Mach 3! Everest's last flight had been his greatest; the speed research frontier had been pushed back another notch.

After his last flight, Pete turned over the X-2 to Kinch, and the powerful rocket craft which had been Everest's plane unofficially for more than two years now became Kincheloe's plane. With the X-2, Everest also turned over to Kinch his little blue Model A, a transfer that was almost an equal honor. Most of the pilots at Edwards had Model A's or T's; they used them to drive to the flight line, leaving the family cars at home for their wives. Pete's blue Model A, though, was a special one, a tradition at the base. It had first belonged to "Chuck" Yeager when he was the Air Force's top test pilot. Yeager had sold it, at the standard rate of one hundred dollars, to the man who would succeed him as "number-one man," Pete Everest. Now the little car, symbolic of top ranking, became Iven Kincheloe's.

There was an uproarious going-away party for Everest. Kinch served as master of ceremonies and he was never better, possibly because he was deliriously happy. He loved and idolized Pete Everest, and he would miss his mentor, but Pete's departure signified the start of a new phase of Kinch's career. He was now the "top rocket man"; he had achieved the goal for which he had pointed so long and worked so hard.

Since Everest had come so close to Mach 3, it was now decided to try for top altitude of 100,000 feet or better, into the space realm. Going for altitude required a different type of flight plan from the speed runs, so before reaching "all the way," the engineers planned a couple of preparatory flights "to check out the X-2's handling characteristics at 85,000 feet before proceeding to the maximum potential altitude."

Kinch flew the first of these preliminary flights on August 3, and his debut as top rocket man was extraordinarily successful, a masterpiece of skill. After the drop, he turned on both rocket chambers and maintained perfectly the predetermined angle of climb up to about 50,000 feet, when the

X-2 was moving at Mach 2 and its rocket power plant still functioning properly.

At 50,000 feet, he encountered "Dutch roll" as the rocket plane wobbled three or four degrees in each direction. Kinch played the controls like the keys of a concert piano and the roll ceased, but he had drifted slightly higher than the programed climb path. Nonetheless, the X-2 continued to climb, its speed still increasing. He topped 70,000 feet, then 75,000. As he approached 85,000 feet at 1,500 miles an hour, the rocket fuel burned out. The X-2 continued to coast upward on its momentum, the speed falling off sharply. At 87,750 feet, just a little more than one thousand feet short of the highest altitude ever attained in an airplane, he was forced to level off. He had reached a top speed of Mach 2.57, about 1,700 miles per hour; he was shy of Everest's speed record, but at the same time, he had climbed the X-2 higher than it had ever been.

The following week he made another preparatory flight, but a premature power shutdown held the X-2 down to 70,000 feet. Nonetheless, it was a successful flight, since no new control problems developed. The X-2 project group got together, studied the results of the last two flights, and concluded it was time to "go for the moon"—to fly the X-2 to the limit of its altitude potential. The plane was taken out of service for another complete rework of its temperamental power system before trying for the "big one," a flight which, if successful, would take Kinch above 100,000 feet and into the fringes of space. The date was set for September 7.

XII. FIRST OF THE SPACEMEN

O_{N THE} morning of September 7, at precisely 6 A.M., the harsh clang of the alarm clock reminded Kinch that this was the Big Day, the day he could go "all out for altitude" and, if everything worked right, climb to a point in the heavens farther from Earth's surfaces than man had ever been before.

The first thing he did on awakening was to check the weather. It was fine. Already the fireball sun was poking up over the San Bernardino foothills and the morning sky was as blue as only a desert sky can be. Kinch smiled with satisfaction.

He shaved, showered, and dressed quickly, and while Dorothy was getting ready, he sipped a glass of milk. He wanted no breakfast. If anything went wrong with the pressure system of the X-2 while he was at high altitude, the less food he had in his system the better off he would be.

They drove to the base together in the Cadillac. Technically, Dorothy was not supposed to witness the flight, but Kinch thought he would feel better if he knew she was down below watching, and it was unlikely that anyone would make an issue of her presence.

It was a couple of minutes before seven when Kinch reported to the Personal Equipment Lab, where the chief, Happy Plaga, and a couple of airmen were waiting to help him into the pressure suit. This was an important piece of equipment on this flight. If anything happened to the cockpit pressurization system at the altitudes Kinch hoped to reach, his blood would boil in the thin upper atmosphere and he would be dead in a matter of seconds without the protection of the suit. In an emergency, the suit, a skintight garment interlaced with rubber tubing, would inflate automatically on first detection of an "explosive decompression" and place ten pounds of pressure over Kinch's entire body to simulate sea-level pressure. At the same time, oxygen would be forced into his sealed helmet to permit him to breathe until he could maneuver to a lower altitude.

Kinch shed his uniform and donned his "long Johns," which would protect his skin against chafing. Then, with the help of Plaga and the airmen, he wriggled into the pressure suit. Plaga tightened the multiple laces and Kinch did a series of knee bends to iron out the kinks.

Next they checked the emergency oxygen bottle attached to Kinch's parachute. In case of a pressure failure, the emergency oxygen would cut in automatically. If, however, Kinch had to "blow the plane apart," he would pull a cord to start the oxygen flow. Blowing the plane apart meant separating the escape capsule from the airplane. At the speeds at which the X-2 would be traveling, the ordinary ejection seat used in jet aircraft would be useless—Kinch would be torn to shreds by the terrific air blast as he left the cockpit. In the X-2, he could blow the entire nose section containing the cockpit away from the rest of the plane by activating an explosive charge. A small parachute would pop out automatically to stabilize the capsule until it slowed to a point where Kinch could bail out safely.

Kinch pulled on his tight-laced flight boots, then Plaga slipped the helmet over his head and affixed the face plate.

"Let's give it a try," he said. He led Kinch to a compressed-air bottle, hooked up the connections, turned the air valve. The rubber tubing inflated properly, tightening the suit and forcing Kinch to bend slightly. Plaga studied the dials on a console panel and made a circle with thumb and forefinger. He turned off the air pressure.

"You're all set as far as I'm concerned," he said as he removed the helmet.

A pickup truck drove Kinch the three miles to South Base, where the X-2 was being readied. The plane site was a scene of hectic activity as more than seventy people scurried about the X-2 and its "mother" ship, the specially converted B-50 which would carry it aloft.

Final preparations had started hours earlier, at 0200, when a group of U.S.A.F., Bell, and National Advisory Committee for Aeronautics technicians had begun last checks of every part of both airplanes. At 0500, they had signified everything in readiness for the "mating." The B-50 was raised on hydraulic jacks and the X-2 rolled into position under it. The mother plane was gradually lowered until the X-2 fitted snugly into the bomb bay, the shackles were connected, the release mechanism tested, and the combined planes towed off to the fuel-loading pit.

Fuel-loading was a two-part operation. The powerful Curtiss-Wright XLR-25 rocket engine burned a combination of alcohol and liquid oxygen in its two rocket tubes, the large one of 10,000 and the smaller one of 5,000 pound thrust. Under pressure, the fuels were forced into the burner chambers by a turbine pump, ignited by a spark plug and—*whoosh!*

At 0630, the fueling crew had started to load the alcohol. Loading of the liquid oxygen, or "lox," was the last item on the preflight schedule, because lox is very difficult to handle. One of the coldest substances known, it boils at 290 degrees *below* zero. Thus, in the normal morning desert temperature of about eighty, it evaporates continually, even while being poured into the tanks. In the time it would take to climb to drop altitude, about half the tank capacity would boil. For this reason, the B-50 was equipped with extra lox tanks, so the X-2 could be "topped off" just prior to drop. It was important that the maximum quantity of lox be crammed into the X-2's tanks, for the amount of lox determined the burning time of the rocket tubes, and even a couple of seconds might make an important difference in the top altitude attainable.

By the time Kinch arrived at the plane site, they had started lox loading. A faint white fog covered the area around the X-2 as the vaporous lox leaked out of faults in the fueling tanks. At the Bell Aircraft truck, a rolling tool shed, supervisor of technicians Jimmy Dunn was directing the lox-loading and last-minute checks over a loudspeaker. Nearby, Captain Fitzhugh "Fuzzy" Fulton and his copilot, Captain Frank Cole, were briefing the crew of the mother plane on emergency procedures. There was one paramount consideration—the X-2, with its load of lox, was potentially explosive, so it must be jettisoned immediately if anything went wrong. If Iven Kincheloe happened to be in it, he was expendable, too—it was one life against the ten in the mother plane.

With the B-50 crew were the chase pilots. For this important flight, Kinch would have some high-ranking help. Primary chase pilot was the Director of Flight Test himself—Colonel Horace Hanes. The secondary chaser was none other than the commanding general of the Test Center, Brigadier

General "Stan" Holtoner. They would fly close formation with the B-50 during its drop run and check the movement of the controls for Kinch, who would not be able to see them, since the cockpit of the X-2 would be tucked into the bomb bay of the B-50. They would also signal when the lox tanks were topped off in the air; they would be able to tell by the stream of vapor pouring out of the overflow tube. After the drop, they would follow the flight path of the X-2 as far as they could, but even their supersonic F-100's were no match for the X-2.

For this mission, there were two additional chase pilots, Kinch's friends from Fighter Branch, Pat Hunerwadel and Jim Carson. They would watch the drop and then proceed, respectively, to Mirage Lake and Harpers Dry Lake. In case Kinch missed the planned landing area at Rogers Dry Lake for any reason, they would pick him up and guide him to one of the alternate touchdown points.

Kinch, in his tight pressure suit, strolled to the Bell truck and poured himself a cup of coffee from the big five-gallon urn. He scanned the sky; only a patch of fleecy cirrus marred the blue. He surveyed the scene around the X-2.

"Well," he said, to no one in particular, "looks as though they haven't found anything wrong yet."

"Relax, dad," said a Bell technician. "Nothing's going wrong."

"We've got it hacked," Kinch replied, as if to reassure himself.

Kinch gulped the last of the coffee, took his kneeboard containing the check list, and moved off from the *Kaffee-klatsch*. He studied carefully, for perhaps the twentieth time in the last twenty-four hours, the detailed, two-hundred-item check list he would have to follow once in the plane. One goof, one switch in the wrong position, could cause an abort.

By eight o'clock, he was satisfied that he knew it as well as he ever would. He walked stiffly to the plane, the pressure suit cramping his movements, and strolled around it aimlessly, as if trying to find something the horde of technicians had overlooked.

"How much longer?" he asked one of the lox loaders.

"Not too long. Ten minutes, maybe." As soon as the lox was loaded, there would be a scramble for the plane and a quick take-off, to save as much as possible of the evaporating lox and simplify the top-off job in the air.

Kinch joined the little huddle of engineers at the rear of the plane. They discussed, again for the twentieth time, the flight plan. The B-50 would climb to the west for about an hour, reaching a point thirty-five miles west of Edwards just before the drop, which would take place near Rogers Dry Lake, the twelve-mile natural runway of sun-baked sand with the consistency of concrete.

Kinch would have about 140 seconds of powered flight after the drop, during which time he would accelerate to more than twice the speed of sound and climb as high as 135,000 feet if everything worked perfectly, if the temperamental engine behaved, if the lox-topping was conducted efficiently, and if Kinch could follow the predetermined flight plan exactly, which would exact the last iota of his incredible skill.

After "burn-out," he would glide back to Rogers Lake for the landing; the regular runways just were not long enough for the hot rocket plane, which would touch the sand at more than 200 miles per hour. The point of drop had to be very precise—close enough to Rogers Lake to permit a quick landing if the engine failed to light, yet not too close, or Kinch would overrun his turning point after burn-out.

One of the big jobs, which would fall to Bell's power-plant

man Bill Fleming, was starting the turbine pump which forced the alcohol and lox into the burners as the B-50 started its drop run. Fleming would have just thirty seconds to do it—after that they would have moved too far for a safe drop. But starting it was a real problem, because of the intensely cold lox which iced up the pump. It was like starting a car on a cold winter morning, except that you had only one, maybe two, shots at the starter.

After the drop, it was up to Kinch to hold the precise speed and angle of climb called for in the flight plan. Any deviation from it would cut down the maximum altitude. He would be aided by radar operators on the ground, who would track his altitude and signal it by coded numeral. "One" meant forty-five thousand feet, and each succeeding number meant another five thousand feet. At "eleven," if he made it, he would be higher than man had ever been.

Happy Plaga came running up with Kinch's helmet under his arm.

"They're nearly finished with the lox," he said. "Let's get this hard hat on."

Kinch slapped on the helmet and shook hands with the engineers. A cloud of vapor billowed up around the X-2, signifying the end of the lox-loading process, as the liquid oxygen spilled out of the overflow pipe. A crewman signaled to Bell's Jimmy Dunn at the loudspeaker.

"Lox loaded. B-50 crew board your plane," Dunn announced. "Bring me back a piece of green cheese, Kinch," he shouted, as Kinch jogged stiffly toward the B-50.

Kinch swung nimbly up the fore hatch and took his seat in the nose of the B-50, between Fulton and Cole, the pilots. Behind him was Fleming, seated at the launch panel, a set of instruments duplicating those in the X-2, enabling him to follow the check list with Kinch and double-check each item.

Aft of the bomb bay, where the X-2 hung, were two N.A.C.A. technicians who would handle the lox-topping, and in the rear were two Air Force sergeants who would serve as scanners, watching the B-50's engines, which the pilots could not see, for oil leaks or other trouble. A flight engineer, Plaga, and one of his assistants rounded out the crew.

A Bell technician took a last look around the X-2 to see that all hoses and wires had been disconnected, then he ran around to the front of the plane to signal the pilots and the driver of the tow truck which would pull the B-50 to the end of the runway. He waved good luck to Kinch in the nose and the tow started to move.

At the end of the runway the tow was unhooked. Fulton already had all four engines running and checked. With a roar, the B-50 started down the runway, lifting easily. It was 0824.

At 2,000 feet, Kinch slipped out of the nose and made his way back to Plaga's station. Plaga slipped on the parachute, checked all the straps, and took a last look at the oxygen bottle. Kinch donned his heavy flight gloves and Plaga sealed them with tape. Plaga slapped the helmet face plate in place, clamped it, and held up thumb and forefinger to signify "All set."

Kinch crawled through the hatch to the bomb bay and dropped down a ladder into the cramped cockpit of the X-2, while Plaga and his assistant took their places on a narrow catwalk, one on either side of the cockpit.

They buckled on shoulder harness and seat belt and plugged in the pressure suit and oxygen connections and the interphone wire. Plaga tapped on Kinch's helmet to indicate everything was in readiness, and the helmet bobbed in acknowledgment. They fitted the canopy in place, then left the bomb bay. Kinch wriggled into as comfortable a position as he could manage in the cockpit which was two sizes too small for him, then started the long check list.

"Oxygen pressure, okay," he called to Fleming at the launch panel. "Engine master switch, off. Radio switch, on." Fleming confirmed each item.

Fulton circled the dry lake, climbing to 20,000 feet while Kinch and Fleming ran through the check list. At 20,000 feet, the chase planes slid into position and reported over the radio, as did the two photographic planes, one on the right wing of the B-50, the other higher up. The formation headed west, toward the drop zone, still climbing.

"Item forty, control check," Kinch droned into the intercom. "Nose down, nose up, going right, going left," as he manipulated the control stick. To each call came the calm reply of Horace Hanes in the chase plane as he checked the movement of the control surfaces. "Nose down, roger."

Fulton, up front in the "office," called to the "back room." "Start lox top-off." The N.A.C.A. technicians moved into the bomb bay and connected the hoses.

The formation passed over the little town of Rosamond and continued west to a point about ten miles past the drop zone. Fulton reported the altitude—25,000 feet—and called for all hands to check in. Then he started a series of figure eights. They were getting close to the tricky part of the operation, the turn onto the drop run, which called for skilled teamwork. The turn, the completion of the lox-topping, and the end of Kinch's check list had to coincide for maximum efficiency in the drop. Fulton had to time his turns so he would be close to the center of a figure eight when it came time to start the drop run. Then it would be Fleming's turn. He had to get the balky turbine pump started at precisely the right second. After that, it was all up to Kinch.

The B-50 droned on, its engines laboring slightly now in

the thin upper air, its contrails streaming behind like fleecy ribbons. In the X-2, Kinch snapped through the litany of the check list, working swiftly yet surely. From various members of the crew came confirmations of each item of the check. On the ground, at listening posts and radar stations, hundreds of people listened in mounting tension as drop time approached.

"Thirty thousand," Fulton reported over the intercom. He exchanged a look with his copilot. The B-50 was climbing better than it usually did and it still had some left. It was a good sign.

He started another half of the figure eight. Thirty-one thousand, thirty-two, and then, with the bomber's engines protesting the strain, thirty-three! They were higher than they had ever been before on an X-2 test, meaning that Kinch would drop higher and get a head start on his altitude run.

Suddenly, from Hanes in the chase plane, as a stream of vapor from the overflow pipe in the X-2 signified full lox tanks:

"Top-off complete!"

"Close top-off switch. Disconnect," Fleming called.

"Roger. Lox-fill hose disconnected," came the reply.

Fulton had already swung into his turn to the east, on the drop run. Kinch was on schedule with the check list. Fleming built up his pressure for a turbine start.

"Two minutes to drop," Fleming announced.

Now the pace of the check list was stepped up as Kinch snapped the various switches to ON and received Fleming's confirmation.

"Minute and a half to drop."

"Roger," from Kinch. "Battery switch on. Selector switch to START."

Now Fulton pushed the B-50 over into a shallow dive to

pick up momentum for the drop, calling out his air speed: "Two twenty—two thirty—two forty—two fifty."

"Got a start!" Fleming yelled as the turbine pump kicked into action. Then: "Ready to drop!"

Fulton reached down by his right knee and pulled the safety pin from the launch handle. "Ready to drop, roger. Air speed two sixty. Start your countdown, Kinch."

"Five—four—three—two—one—drop it!" It was an exciting moment for Iven Kincheloe, the start of a venture into an altitude realm that man had never before explored; yet, from the sound of his voice, low-pitched, calm, and assured, the listeners on the ground and in the other planes might think he was taking a ride on a merry-go-round. His voice belied his feelings. As he described it later, he had a sinking feeling in the pit of his stomach, like the gnawing of a hunger pain. He knew only too well the dangers of the mission he was about to start, but the knowledge was crowded into a back corner of his brain. Through his conscious mind whipped the long list of things he must do in the next few minutes, and do perfectly. He was tense but exhilarated.

Fulton pulled the handle, the shackles popped open, and the little white rocket ship was dropping. It was 0915.

The big, 10,000-pound-thrust rocket tube started with a streak of flame as Kinch slammed home the throttle. The instant acceleration pushed him back in his seat. Over the radio came Hanes's reassurance: "Ten's going good." Kinch snapped on the other tube, the 5,000-pounder, and the second flash of flame blended with the first. "Five's going good."

Rocket tubes spewing a long trail of fire, the X-2 roared upward, rapidly losing the B-50 and the chase planes. Kinch was busy, deftly manipulating the controls, trying to watch all the instruments at once. Despite the angle of his climb, his speed was increasing at an incredible rate. In a matter of seconds, he topped Mach 1, the speed of sound.

Now the radar unit added its voice to the radio chorus. "We've got you. Up—up—up—*one*." He had reached the first check point, 45,000 feet, right on flight plan.

The X-2 sped on in the climb, its contrail streaking across the sky like a quick chalk stroke on a blackboard. The only noise was the rush of the outside air as it swirled around the nose and over the cockpit.

"Up—up—up—*five*." Sixty-five thousand feet and the mighty little rocket plane still had plenty left. Kinch was still "right on" the preplanned climb schedule. The plane was handling perfectly.

Kinch called off the instrument readings and described the flight characteristics of the X-2 as he continued to climb. There was a little buffeting on the wings, not much, not enough to worry about. His comments were being recorded on tape for later study. In addition, a special set of instruments was recording research data, and a camera, pointed over his shoulder at the cockpit panel in front of him, was photographing the instrument readings and noting on film the precise time of each reading by taking a matching picture of a sensitive clock which displayed the time in fractions of a second.

"*Ten!*" shouted the radarman, his voice no longer toneless. Kinch and the X-2 had just passed 90,000 feet. Kinch, sweating now with tension and exertion, permitted himself a broad smile. He could almost hear the hurrahs from the watchers on the ground and he could visualize Dorothy's happy smile. He had just topped the previous altitude record, set by Major Kit Murray in another Bell rocket plane two years earlier.

But the X-2 was by no means done. It still had a few seconds of rocket power left and it was still going up—and fast. He was doing better than 1,500 miles an hour, more than twice the speed of a rifle bullet, and with every second he was barreling farther into the virgin territory of space.

He passed 100,000 feet and with a dying rumble the rocket tubes consumed the last of their fuel and quit, 133 seconds after Kinch had hit the throttle, although it seemed much longer.

The X-2 continued upward after burn-out, coasting in eerie silence on its momentum. Kinch was in space, the first of the spacemen, if you accepted the arbitrary border line of 100,000 feet set by some experts. At that altitude, almost 100 per cent of the earth's atmosphere was beneath the X-2. There was no air to support flight; it was climbing on momentum alone. The sun's rays, unfiltered by the atmosphere which protects earth-bound man from their brilliance, were intensely bright, so blinding that he could not see the pad affixed to his knee on which he was scribbling notes. Away from the sun, the space sky was a deep purple.

Now the X-2 began to slow down, not much in terms of miles per hour, for he was still moving at more than 1,000 miles per hour, but there was a noticeable slackening of momentum and the plane became slightly sluggish. It started to roll a little; Kinch ignored it. Still climbing, but less rapidly, he passed the 120,000-foot level, then 125,000. Later, radar computed the precise zenith of his parabolic flight path: 126,200 feet!

At the top of the ride, Kinch allowed himself a brief look out of the canopy. Far below, he could see the brown earth of the desert and he could make out a railroad track, looking like a pencil line on a relief map. He could clearly see the curvature of the earth, accentuating the feeling of being in space. Far to the west, he could see the waters of the Pacific Ocean through a misty blue haze; his awed gaze carried hundreds of miles in any direction. He took one last look at the purplish black of the space void above him, and then the X-2 was starting down, picking up new speed as it was relieved of the strain of climbing and gravity pulled him back toward earth.

He plummeted downward in a near-vertical dive, gaining speed rapidly. The needle of his Machmeter crept up past 2, then 2.5. He was below 100,000 feet now, officially back on earth, though a long way from its surface. The needle hit 2.6, more than 1,700 miles an hour, faster than the mighty rockets had pushed the X-2 on the way out. Then, as he dove into the heavier atmosphere, he flattened out the descent curve and the plane slowed down.

Now he was gliding easily, under the speed of sound, in the general direction of Rogers Dry Lake, where he would land, though he could not yet see it. He was terribly weary; the tension had drained him of his strength, but he exulted in a feeling of accomplishment. He felt relaxed, dreamy.

The voice of chase pilot Jim Carson on the radio brought him back to reality. "I've got you, Kinch." They were at 50,000 feet.

Carson slipped into position on the X-2's wing tip and gave Kinch a "steer" to the dry lake. They chatted easily over the radio as they headed for it. Carson radioed instructions to line the X-2 up for the landing and Kinch held it at a steady 240 miles an hour, the X-2's best gliding speed. It was still tricky, for with no power there would be only one shot at the landing, but Kinch maneuvered the plane neatly into position. The controls, as if glad to have some air to work with, responded perfectly and then the landing skids which took the place of wheels touched lightly on the runway, spewing up a geyser of sand as the X-2 slid for a mile or so.

The plane slowed to a halt and a stream of cars and trucks

and jeeps carrying the "welcoming committee" sped out to the runway. Kinch sat limp in the cockpit.

Then eager hands were removing the canopy and others helped Kinch out of the plane. He was tired, and sweating profusely. Someone took off his helmet and someone else was undoing the lacing of the tight pressure suit. The jubilant welcoming committee was pounding him on the back, shouting, "You did it, boy!"

Over their heads he saw Dorothy smiling at him. He elbowed his way through the crowd and kissed her lightly. Then he turned back to his well-wishers.

Kinch wrote his report on the flight the following day. In typical Kincheloe fashion, it was terse and succinct, two paragraphs to describe man's greatest flight to that date. The closing sentence was a masterpiece of understatement:

"The aircraft was pleasant to fly throughout the flight and the achievement as anticipated."

XIII. PLANNING THE ALL-OUT SPEED RUN

As far as the X-2 program was concerned, the next few weeks were uneventful. Kinch held a post-flight conference in which he described to a gathering of engineers connected with the program the technical details of his record flight. His notes, scribbled hastily on the knee pad during the flight, were transcribed, as was the radio tape. The cockpit-camera film was removed from the plane and developed for detailed study. The data from the research-instrument package was fed into an automatic computer for analysis. For weeks, the scientists and engineers would be digesting all this information. Then they would collate it into a comprehensive study of the behavior of man and his machine in a completely new flight regime. The volume would be a significant addition to the library of man's aeronautical knowledge.

The next flight of the X-2 had been scheduled for September 11, but it was postponed several times because of minor difficulties. The Bell and Air Force technicians had given the X-2 a thorough going-over after Kinch's altitude run, and it was in good shape, but there were always a hundred little things going wrong, like the turbine pump or the lox-loading equipment, or maybe only the research instrumentation.

These instruments had nothing to do with the operation of either the B-50 or the X-2; they merely recorded data. However, at Edwards they were as important as any item of flight equipment. The Air Force was not conducting the X-2 program to set a series of records for publicity purposes. The goal was knowledge, a thorough understanding of conditions and problems in new areas of speed and altitude, which would be used to build better-performing, more efficient military aircraft later on. The X-2 was purely and simply a research tool, and if the data-recording instruments were not functioning, there was no point in running the mission at all.

The next flight would fall to Mel Apt. Mel was a thoroughly experienced pilot and a grade-A aeronautical engineer, but he had never flown a rocket-powered airplane. There were good reasons, though, for putting him into the X-2 program even at this advanced stage.

For one thing, the Air Force needed another rocket man. Yeager, Everest, Murray, and the few others who had rocket experience had all been transferred and Kinch was now the only qualified U.S.A.F. rocket pilot. General Holtoner, the Test Center commander, and his bosses in Baltimore wanted to check out another good rocket man. There was a new rocket program in the mill, and Kinch could not be expected to carry it alone. Aside from the work load it would entail, there was always the possibility of an accident involving Kincheloe. Testing advanced aircraft like the X-2 was probably the most dangerous job in the world, and if anything happened to Kinch, the rocket-research program would grind to a halt until the tedious and time-consuming business of training a replacement could be accomplished. For another thing, the X-2 was now the only rocket plane available to the Air Force and it would soon have to give up that. Under the original agreement, the U.S.A.F. was to operate the airplane for a given period of time to explore the "envelope" in broad outline, that is, to boost its performance over a series of flights up to the maximum possible speed and altitude. Then the airplane was to be turned over to the National Advisory Committee for Aeronautics, which would, over a longer period, fill in the research gaps not covered by the Air Force.

The long series of delays with the X-2 had pushed the transfer date back farther and farther, and now N.A.C.A. was pressing to get the airplane. It was agreed that the U.S.A.F. could make one more flight, an attempt to go "all out for speed," then the X-2 would be turned over to N.A.C.A.

So, if the U.S.A.F. was to check out a new rocket man, it would have to be on the next, and for the Air Force the last, flight of the X-2.

This brought up another problem. No one questioned Mel Apt's ability. He had thousands of flying hours and a great many of them in jets and he had flown practically all of the experimental aircraft at Edwards. But could he, with no rocket time, fly the very precise flight path required to attain the maximum speed potential of the X-2? Would it not be better to go with Kincheloe, who had a better chance of filling in the speed portion of the research envelope?

The answer, the Test Center supervisors agreed, was that, sure, Kinch would probably be the better choice and Apt's chances of reaching "max" were slim. But Pete Everest had flown the plane to a speed of Mach 2.87, almost 1,900 miles per hour, pretty close to max. If Apt failed to better that, the data from Everest's flight would stand as interim max and N.A.C.A. could make another top-speed try later. If, by some miracle, Apt should fly a perfect flight plan, that was frosting on the cake. The most important immediate goal was the checking out of a new rocket man.

So Apt got the assignment, to Kinch's disappointment. He would have liked to have made the speed run, too, but he was a realist. He knew as well as anyone the importance of having a "back-up" rocket pilot and he liked and respected Mel Apt and wanted him to succeed.

Kinch's end of the assignment was to coach Mel for his maiden rocket flight and he plunged into it with characteristic vigor. Apt was by no means unversed in rocket flight. For eight months he had been getting ready. He had explored every inch of the plane itself; he had spent long hours with the engineers, absorbing details of its construction and operation; he had studied carefully the data from each of Everest's and Kinch's flights, watched hours of research film, checked over the rocket power plant and its intricate works, investigated in detail each of the plane's complicated systems, and worked a great many hours in the X-2 simulator. He knew almost as much about the X-2 as did Kinch or any of the engineers—so much, he said, that he felt "he could build it from memory."

But he had not flown it, and that was Kinch's job: to impart to Mel all the knowledge of the handling characteristics of the little "beast" it was possible to transfer from one mind to another. Together they inspected the plane, its engine, and all its systems, worked in the simulator, and discussed a hundred times over every sequence of an X-2 mission.

The repeated postponements of the flight gave them extra time. Kinch worked hard at his job of tutelage. Sometimes, in the middle of a staff meeting, he would stop and jot down a note to himself—some minor little item he must remember to pass on to Mel. He was literally trying to project his accumulated rocket experience into Mel Apt's brain, as he had so often before absorbed knowledge from others.

Finally, in late September, they got the word that the flight was "on." The X-2 was ready, the B-50 was ready, the support equipment, the systems, and the research instruments had all been "debugged." September 25 was to be the Big Day.

Then Public Relations in the Pentagon stepped into the act. Although word of Kinch's altitude record had not yet been officially released, Kinch was already a minor celebrity as the U.S.A.F.'s top test pilot, and the Pentagon press agents, who were close to the "brass" and could make such things stick, had decided that Kinch should represent the Air Force at the première of a new motion picture about test pilots. The movie, titled *Toward the Unknown* from the motto of the Flight Test Center, was to be premièred in Baltimore.

All over the base, there were some explosive comments hurled at Pentagon stupidity, press agents, and movie-makers in general; the X-2 mission order stipulated that Apt would not fly without Kincheloe as chase, since it was up to Kinch to coach Mel into the initial flight attitude for his speed run. Mel Apt, who should have been most upset about the delay, took it calmly. He joked about it.

"Here I am all set to go to the moon and he has to go see a movie."

The X-2 group had to bow to superior authority and the "all out for speed" mission was set back two days to permit Kinch to streak to Baltimore and back. Kinch made the première and dashed back to Edwards in time for the pre-mission briefing with Bell Aircraft, the N.A.C.A., and the Air Force X-2 group on the eve of the flight.

"How was the movie?" someone asked him.

"I learned a lot," Kinch said dryly.

XIV. LAST FLIGHT OF THE X-2

THE DAY of September 27 dawned as brightly as had the day of Kinch's altitude flight. When Kinch awoke about 6 A.M., the weather was perfect. There were a few small patches of cirrus to the east; to the west, the direction from which a slight wind was blowing, there was nothing but cerulean blue. The sun shone brightly on the desert sands.

Kinch was happy about the weather. We ought to go today, he thought. Although he was only a supporting member of the cast for this mission and not the star, he was as interested in it as he had been in his own spectacular trip three weeks earlier.

His supporting role, though, was an important one. He had passed on to Mel Apt all the know-how the latter could possibly assimilate, but he still had one big job left, aside from the routine of flying chase. A vital factor in the success of the speed run would be the initial attitude of the X-2 after the drop, that is, the angle at which Mel pointed it as he turned on the power. Kinch would fly under the wing of the B-50 and radio instructions to help Mel coax the little rocket ship into the proper attitude. From there on, Kinch could do little

127

but watch, and not much of that because the X-2 would pull rapidly away from his jet chase plane.

Kinch rattled down Fitzgerald Boulevard, the main street of the Edwards housing area, in his newly acquired blue Model A. It was almost seven when he reached the gate of the restricted area. Mel was already there, he noted. There was no mistaking Mel's 1931 Model A, which was parked near the gate. When he had first acquired the old car, Mel had appealed to the Personal Equipment Branch for some left-over helmet paint. They didn't have enough of a single color, but they were willing to give him the remains of six partly used cans. This didn't bother Mel at all—he sprayed on all six colors, which, together with some of the original green, gave him the only seven-tone car at Edwards, maybe anywhere.

Kinch checked in at Operations and found everything was still going well. At 0500, he was told, they had finished mating the X-2 and the B-50, and the alcohol had already been loaded. They were about ready to start lox-loading. Mel Apt, in his pressure suit, was already at the plane site.

Kinch donned his own flying suit and rode over to South Base. A glance at the scene around the X-2 told him things were still all right, even before he asked for confirmation. It was not that people jump up and down or tear their hair when something goes wrong, but after long association with the X-2 project, Kinch had a "feel" for it and had there been a "hold," he would have known it instinctively.

Mel Apt was standing by the Bell truck, a cup of coffee in one hand and a doughnut in the other. Like Kinch, Mel ate no big breakfast before a test flight, but he didn't like the "empty" feeling, either. A doughnut was his compromise.

Kinch waved a greeting to Apt and joined the B-50 crew, huddled near the mated planes. Captain Fitzhugh "Fuzzy" Fulton was just starting the briefing. With the crew was Jim

Carson, who would be the other chase pilot. Kinch, as coach, would fly low chase in formation with the B-50; Carson would be "upstairs," about 15,000 feet above the bomber, flying high chase in a supersonic F-100. His added altitude and the greater speed of the F-100 would permit him to stay with the X-2 a few seconds longer after it streaked away from Kinch.

The briefing over, Kinch strolled over to Apt, who was talking to one of the engineers. He clapped his hand on Mel's shoulder and said:

"You've got it hacked, dad." You just didn't say things like "Good Luck," particularly not on the thirteenth powered flight of the X-2, although neither Kinch nor Apt was superstitious.

As Kinch moved away, toward his own plane, the white fog swelled up under the belly of the B-50, and almost simultaneously the loudspeaker boomed, "Lox loaded. B-50 crew, board your plane."

Kinch spent a few minutes walking around his F-86 chase plane, inspecting control surfaces, landing gear, and the other components that were externally visible. He stood talking with the crew chief as the B-50, with the X-2 tucked under its fuselage, rolled down the runway and lifted into the air. He still had plenty of time. He was to join the formation at 20,000 feet and it would take the lumbering bomber about half an hour to get up there. It was now 0748.

A few minutes past eight, Kinch climbed into the cockpit and started his engine, which kicked into life with a howling whine. He ran through the check list, then slowly taxied out to the runway. At another stand, Carson was preparing to move his F-100.

Kinch called in to the tower, pushed his throttle forward, and rolled down the runway. The jet lifted easily and he reached for the gear handle. As the wheels retracted into their wells with a light jolt, he took a look upward and spotted the B-50, its contrails streaming behind as Fulton circled the lake. He pointed the F-86 on an intercept course.

He was precisely at 20,000 feet when he slid into position to the left and below the B-50.

"Low chase, in position," he reported. Over the radio he heard Fulton's "Roger" and then, in succession, Carson and the photo planes checked in. Kinch waited for his cues as Mel Apt rattled through the check list. When Mel reached "control check," Kinch checked each movement of the X-2's control surfaces and reported to Apt.

Now it was 0845 and the formation was above 30,000 feet. From the overflow pipe came the stream of vapor, and Kinch reported: "Top-off complete." Fulton turned to the east, on the drop run.

As Mel started his countdown, Kinch moved in closer. Mel's voice on the radio climbed to a high pitch as he yelled, "Drop it!" The X-2 separated from the bomber, Kinch watching it intently. Rocket flame shot from the exhaust as Apt switched on the 10,000-pound-thrust tube.

"Start the nose up, Mel," Kinch coached. "Ten's going good." There was the second streak of flame. "Five's going now." Mel was handling the plane well. He didn't need much coaching, Kinch noted. "You've got her. Attaboy. Keep her coming back. Some more. You've got her. Looking real good. O. K. He's starting to climb now, high chase."

Kinch applied full throttle to his F-86, but the little rocket plane sped away from him. His part of the job was over until he picked Mel up for the approach.

In the X-2, Mel Apt had little time to think about anything but holding the precise flight path demanded for top speed. The plan called for a parabolic arc, with a rapid climb from drop altitude to 70,000, then a dive to attain the maximum possible Mach number.

Radar's "One" told Mel he was right on flight plan. He was already past Mach 1 and the Machmeter needle was climbing fast. The "two"—50,000 feet—seemed to follow almost instantaneously.

His brain was absorbing the information from all the panel dials at once and translating it into gentle control movements. Now he was past Mach 2 and the needle was still creeping upward. *"Five,"* said radar.

Mel, casting a quick glance at the sensitive altimeter, anticipated the *"six"*—70,000 feet—by a fraction of a second. He pushed over into the dive and the X-2, gravity aiding its mighty rocket push, spurted ahead even faster. The Mach needle reached 3, passed it. He was flying faster than man had ever flown before, faster even than some missiles, 2,060 miles per hour, or almost thiry-five miles a minute!

One hundred and forty seconds after he had applied power, the engine gobbled the last of its fuel and quit with a rumble. In a calm voice, Mel spoke into the intercom.

"O. K. She's cut out. I'm turning." The time of turn was important. He was speeding away from Rogers Lake at a terrific rate, and if he went too far, he might not be able to reach the lake on the return glide.

Suddenly, the intercom listeners heard the calm voice rise to an almost unintelligible shriek.

"She goes—!"

The plane had become violently uncontrollable. Its nose was pitching up sharply, yawing from side to side at the same time. The X-2 rolled over on its back, righted itself and rolled again. Mel was tossed wildly about the cockpit despite the restraining straps. His head slammed against the side of the canopy, then he was jerked to the other side. He fought the controls without effect.

It was a moment for quick decision. No one had ever used the escape capsule before. No one had ever attempted an escape at such speed. But the plane was losing altitude rapidly and at any second Mel might be buffeted into unconsciousness. Mel made his decision and reached for the handle that would blow the capsule off, but a violent lurch pulled him away from it. The plane was hurtling earthward rapidly, still gyrating. He reached again. This time his gloved hand caught the handle. He yanked.

There was a sharp report as the explosive charge severed the connections between cockpit and afterbody. The capsule, momentarily unstabilized in the swift air stream, tumbled end over end, slamming Mel backward and forward, subjecting his body to tremendous "G" forces, shooting a rush of blood to his brain.

With a snap, the trailing parachute billowed out and righted the capsule, but it was too late for Mel Apt; he sagged unconscious in the seat. The parachute, designed only for stability, was too small to lower the capsule gently. It dropped heavily, the 'chute practically useless. With a sickening crash it slammed into the desert floor, nose down, then rolled over on its side. It had been only three minutes earlier that Mel had shouted, "Drop it!"

Cruising in the F-86, Kinch scanned the blue sky for a trace of the rocket plane. It was nowhere in sight. The intercom silence was ominous.

"Mel, can you read me, Mel?" he called.

"Call out your position, Mel," Jim Carson added.

Silence.

"Radar, do you have him?" Kinch asked, then, plaintively, "He's got to be around here somewhere."

Kinch, checking his fuel gauge, started another circle, still scanning the sky. Then, reluctantly, he switched his gaze to the desert floor.

At drop plus fifteen, his voice very low, Kinch spoke into the intercom:

"This is an absolute emergency. Please alert all available aircraft for search."

His fuel was nearly gone. Taking one last look around, he headed back toward the base. There he learned what had happened. Fulton had spotted the capsule from the air and directed a ground unit to the scene. A medic had been flown over by helicopter, but there was nothing he could do. Mel Apt was dead. The X-2 program was over.

XV. A NEW ASSIGNMENT— THE X-15

THE WEEKS following Mel Apt's fatal accident in the X-2 were dismal ones for Kinch. He felt deeply about Apt's loss; he had liked the little "baldy" with the ready grin, and they had been together constantly during the weeks Kinch had spent coaching Mel. He couldn't help wondering, too, whether he had overlooked something in his tutoring of Mel, something Mel should have known to help him in his emergency. A thorough investigation of the accident relieved his mind, for it disclosed that there was nothing Mel or Kinch or anyone could have done once the airplane started its wild gyrating. Mel was a casualty of a research program that would take its toll as long as man wanted to explore the unknown. There was some solace in the fact that the data obtained from Mel's flight was extremely valuable. He had been the first man ever to fly at three times the speed of sound, and the data-recording instruments recovered from the wreckage of the airplane plus the information sent back to the ground during flight would help make that speed regime safe for the next generation of aircraft.

Kinch also felt the loss of the little white research plane, which he had come to love as one loves another human. It had been the only plane of its breed, a great airplane despite the myriad problems that were always cropping up, one which had played a very important role in flight and space research. Now it was gone.

There was a ray of sunshine on the horizon. The X-2 would not be the last of the rocket planes. Already a new one, one of even greater promise, was under construction at the Los Angeles plant of North American Aviation. The new ship was called the X-15 and it offered performance which dwarfed even that of the fabulous X-2. Where the X-2 had had 15,000 pounds of thrust in its rocket tubes, the X-15 would have 60,000. The X-2 had topped 2,000 miles an hour; the X-15 would be able to do better than 4,000. And where Kinch had milked every ounce of performance from the X-2 to get it up to a twenty-four-mile altitude, the X-15 would be able to soar twice as far into space.

In late 1956, details of the X-15 were still secret, but Kinch learned enough from the grapevine to know that he had to be in the cockpit when the X-15 took off into space. That, however, was at least three years away.

In the meantime, he settled back into the less dramatic areas of flight research. He worked simultaneously on a number of projects involving the 100 series of supersonic aircraft, and took on an evaluation of a new one, the Grumman F11F, a Navy carrier-based airplane that Kinch liked better than some of his own service's aircraft.

It wasn't all flying routine. The formal announcement of Kinch's brief venture into space had made him an overnight celebrity. For public relations purposes, he had to spend a lot of his time on the "roast-beef circuit," speaking or taking a bow at the interminable cycle of aviation dinners, lunches, symposia, and conventions. He made radio and television appearances, sat for newspaper and magazine interviews, answered countless letters from people who collected autographs and from school children who now counted him among the idols he once worshiped. Curiously, the fame fell a little flat. He valued it for whatever assistance it might be in furthering his career, but otherwise he was little impressed by his own importance.

During this period, the Kincheloe Master Plan broadened. He had always been interested in the possibilities of space flight, and his brief exposure to it had whetted his appetite. Where he had been a space enthusiast, he now became a fanatic, because, always the visionary, he could see the day drawing closer when man would take significant steps into space. He wanted to be among the first, and when his testing days were through, he wanted to have a hand in the planning for later astronautic ventures.

With these goals in mind, he started again his characteristic approach of reading and brain-picking, sending away for every paper on space flight he heard of, and devoting all of his attention at the various meetings he attended to the men who were already studying the engineering, physiological, and psychological problems of putting man in space.

He had little time for home life, what with his flying and the "roast-beef circuit," but he spent every spare minute he could get at home with Dorothy. They had their own stucco Wherry rambler now, and he built a cement patio in the back, engraving it with a huge heart pierced by the traditional arrow, embroidered with his and Dorothy's initials. He liked to putter about the lawn or tinker with his Model A; it was about all the relaxation he got.

His travels kept him constantly broke, for although the Air Force paid a small per-diem allowance for trips away from Edwards, this rarely covered half the actual cost. For Christmas that year, 1956, he could buy Dorothy only a wine-bottle opener, a kitchen stool, and a pair of earrings. He was always buying her earrings, even if he only had a dollar left on one of his trips. They were sort of a token of apology for the time he was forced to spend away from her.

January 9 was Dorothy's birthday and they had planned a little private celebration. The day before, he jumped off the wing of an airplane and injured his back, but no one ever knew it until after the birthday party, though Kinch looked pale and ill. The following day, he checked into the hospital and spent five days there, fidgeting all the time because he missed his airplanes.

March 31, 1957, was another big day in the life of Iven Kincheloe. He became a father. They named the baby boy Robert, but Kinch liked "Sam" better. After visiting Dorothy in the hospital and taking his first look at his red-faced off-spring, he bought twenty-five dollars' worth of the traditional supplies and went careering around the housing area in his Model A, knocking on every door, thrusting a cigar or a piece of candy at the startled occupant and shouting:

"It's a boy and he's got ears like mine."

In July it was announced that Iven Kincheloe was the recipient of the Air Force's Mackay Trophy "for the most meritorious flight of the preceding year." The following month, he and Dorothy and General Marcus Cooper, who had replaced Stan Holtoner as commander of the Test Center, journeyed to Washington for the presentation at the annual convention of the Air Force Association. It was a great thrill to Kinch to accept the award from his "big boss," Air Force Chief of Staff General Thomas D. White.

And in September came another thrill, another step in the Master Plan. It had come time to pick a pilot for the X-15, for although the plane would not be ready for flight until

1958 at the earliest, it demanded the most exacting type of handling and the pilot must undergo a long and strenuous period of training.

This time Kinch "had it hacked." There was little debate as to who would get the assignment. Kinch's exploits and ability were well known to General Cooper and his top advisers and, moreover, he was the only active Air Force test pilot with rocket experience. He was named project test pilot, with Captain Bob White as his alternate.

The X-15 assignment touched off a new round of frantic activity. He had first to learn everything known about the airplane, from drawing-board design to its handling characteristics. Once or twice every week, he would visit the Los Angeles plant of North American Aviation, check on the progress of the program, brain-pick the scientists and engineers working on it, and fly the simulator. The simulator was a complete cockpit of the X-15, with an electronic system whereby he could duplicate the flight conditions to be encountered on any type of planned X-15 mission, from a simple check-out to a parabolic trip fifty miles into space. He was delighted to find that the cockpit was a nice big, roomy one, permitting even a full stretch of his long legs.

Then there was the centrifuge. When eventually Kinch poured full power to the X-15, he would encounter terrific "acceleration forces" which would press him back in his seat with the same effect as if several times his own weight were placed on his chest. Such severe "G" forces—up to ten times the normal pull of gravity—would restrict his movements and interfere with his general efficiency in handling the airplane. Yet the airplane required extremely precise piloting, so the pilot must become accustomed to the body pulls.

At Johnsville, Pennsylvania, the Navy had a machine to duplicate the high "G" forces. Called a centrifuge, it was a merry-go-round type of contrivance with a capsule attached to one end of a long arm. By rotating the capsule at ever-increasing speed, the acceleration forces could be reproduced.

Kinch and Bob White spent long hours in the centrifuge, and it was rough training as the capsule picked up speed and the forces squeezed their bodies down in the seat, rendering them almost helpless. On one such experiment, Kinch pulled so many "G's" that he returned to Edwards with bruises all over his body and had to be hospitalized for observation. Gradually, though, he learned how to resist the high acceleration loads and perform at least simple control maneuvers.

He participated in a number of space physiological experiments at Lovelace Clinic, designed to determine his reactions to a number of odd conditions he would encounter in space, and he flew a series of "weightless" flights. When the X-15 roared into space, Kinch would literally be weightless for a few minutes, as he had been for a few seconds in the X-2. This phenomenon, about which little was known, also posed a potential threat to his ability to handle the X-15. It was possible to duplicate the condition for very brief periods by flying high-speed aircraft in a precise parabolic path, re-creating in miniature the path the X-15 would take.

The constant round of travel, training, speaking engagements, conferences with X-15 project people, television appearances, and interviews was placing a terrific strain on Iven Kincheloe. He was now doubly famous, as the man who had first crossed the threshold of space in the X-2 and as the man who would get the first significant look at space in the X-15. Yet despite all the time and effort his public-relations work and his X-15 training took, he had to keep up his less spectacular job testing operational and near-operational aircraft.

In March, 1958, the Air Force formalized his role as top space man by creating a new section under Flight Test Operations called the Manned Spacecraft Branch. Kinch was named chief of the section and given as assistants Bob White and another pilot from Fighter Branch, Captain Bob Rushworth, a big guy similar in build and general appearance to Kinch himself.

That same month he got a brief respite from the "roast-beef circuit." Along with several others from the Air Force and N.A.C.A. X-15 project groups, he was ordered to France to fly some French experimental aircraft, primarily the Trident and the Griffon, which had certain characteristics in common with the X-15 although their performance capabilities nowhere approached those of the rocket ship under construction.

When he returned late in April, he found he had received another award, the Air Force Association's Air Progress Award. Dorothy had accepted it at a dinner in Los Angeles.

Early in June, he got his first look at the completed X-15, completed, that is, from the standpoint of the airframe, although a lot of work remained to be done on the power-plant installation and a number of the complicated systems. It was a beautiful plane, sleek and powerful in appearance, with a long fuselage and short, stubby wings. He could hardly wait to climb in that wonderfully roomy cockpit and blast "out of this world." He was impatient with the builders, although he knew as well as anyone that it takes time and patience to construct such an intricate, complex vehicle with the performance they were designing into it.

On the same trip to Los Angeles, he performed an interesting space experiment. To learn about the vacuum-like conditions of space, a Los Angeles research firm named Litton Industries had constructed the first real vacuum chamber. Kinch, still thirsting for knowledge, had convinced General Cooper that it would help his X-15 work if he could go into the chamber, test the special space suit built for survival in it, and investigate his own reactions in a simulated environment of one hundred miles from the surface of the earth.

The chamber was a long cylindrical tank with an air lock on one side, through which the "subject" entered, and a series of console panels on the other, where a gaggle of instruments monitored the pressure in the space suit and the subject's physiological reaction. There was an observation port for the flight surgeon, who would watch for danger signals, for if anything happened to the space suit, Kinch would be exposed to the vacuum of space in which he could survive only for seconds.

It took an hour and a half to pump the air out of the chamber and reduce its pressure to the equivalent of one hundred miles' altitude. During this time, Kinch was briefed on the operation of the tank and fitted with the space suit, a bulky metal-and-rubber garment with hinged arms and legs and a massive helmet. After testing arm and leg movements, which were extremely difficult, he breathed pure oxygen for a few minutes to get the nitrogen out of his system, for the nitrogen could cause "bends" if there was even a minor loss of presure in the space suit.

Kinch spent two hours in the chamber, testing his own mobility and psychological reactions under realistic space conditions. Wired for pulse beat, heart action, respiration, and blood pressure, he performed simple experiments like walking, stooping, using various tools and manipulating a set of clamps on a laboratory table. Toward the end of his test, when he had become used to the restrictions of the space suit, he managed to thread a needle despite his huge gloves and the difficulty of moving his arms. He came out of the chamber smiling, convinced that with proper training man could operate in space, thrilled with his accomplishment of living two hours at one hundred miles' altitude, even though he had never left the ground.

And then it was back to the road for another go at the centrifuge in Johnsville, a visit to Dayton where the X-15 pressure suit was under development, and another public-relations date.

XVI. THE END OF THE DREAM

THE MORNING of July 26, 1958, dawned beautifully. The early temperature was eighty-six degrees, visibility was fifteen miles, and the wind was calm. It was a good day for flying.

Although it was Saturday, Kinch had a mission to fly—a chase mission, of all things, but someone had to do them. Although he was now chief of Manned Spacecraft, there were not as yet any manned spacecraft to fly, so Kinch was keeping up his routine work with Fighter Branch. Since he was traveling most of the time and since Fighter Branch was always short-handed, Kinch was never averse to taking a Saturday flight to take the work load off some of the others.

He didn't feel like taking this one, though. He was weary, thoroughly fatigued. He had been pushing too hard, he knew, and he thought he would have to slow down the pace.

He had just returned from a trip East on Thursday, and that night he had presided at a meeting of the Antelope Valley Branch of the American Rocket Society, of which he was vice-president and incoming president. Yesterday, Friday, he had flown in the afternoon and in the evening had sat around for hours hangar-flying with Pat Hunerwadel and Jean Franchi, the Frenchman who had gone through test-pilot school with Kinch and who was paying a short visit to Edwards. He had slept badly, too, restless from overfatigue.

As he rolled toward the base in his black Cadillac, he thought how glad he would be to get this one over with. He wanted to get home and see Dorothy. They had not had much time together lately and she was pregnant again; the new baby would be along in a couple of months. Little "Sam" had become one of the great joys of Kinch's life, and it would be nice to have another one padding about. And he had to fix up the patio today, too; he was planning a *luau* party.

Despite the rough grind of the past few months, things were looking pretty good for Iven Kincheloe. He was broke but happy; he had three cars, a nice little home, and a family he loved more than airplanes. His promotion to major ought to come through soon and the X-15 would roll out of its construction hangar in a couple of months. What more could a man want?

He checked into Operations, donned his flying suit and reported to Steve Elliott, the civilian dispatcher. Elliott outlined the mission, a contractor chase for a Lockheed F-104A. Kinch would also fly an F-104, No. 772, which he had flown a number of times during phase tests. The F-104 was a hot airplane, with great "zoomability" as Kinch called it—the ability to climb rapidly. It was a balky airplane, though, and there had been considerable trouble with it.

Kinch generally liked the airplane's performance, but there were a couple of things he and the other pilots did not especially like. For one thing, the plane had a glide angle like the Washington Monument; if it lost power, it would drop like a rock, because it was a heavy airplane and its

144

stubby wings were built for high speed, not gliding. For another thing, its ejection seat fired downward instead of upward, which was fine at high altitude but not so good for a low-altitude ejection; you would have to roll it upside down before hitting the panic button—if you had time. Its engine, too, was temperamental.

Today's mission would take only thirty or forty minutes, starting about 9 A.M. The pilot who would perform the test for Lockheed was none other than Lou Schalk, Kinch's old friend from Fighter Branch and collaborator on his theatrical productions. Schalk had resigned from the Air Force several months earlier to become a civilian test pilot for Lockheed.

Schalk's test plane was based at Lockheed's hangar at Palmdale, another test base sixty miles south of Edwards, so tester and chase would have to rendezvous in the air. Schalk was waiting for a call from the chase pilot to set up the details, Elliott told Kinch.

Kinch got Schalk on the phone.

"What's the matter?" he greeted his old friend. "Can't you make enough money on a five-day week?"

"Fancy hearing your voice," Schalk replied. "To what do I owe this honor? Are you in town over the weekend and slumming with the chase missions?"

Kinch kept up the banter.

"I needed a few hours for flight pay," he said. "With all my junketing, it's hard to squeeze it in."

"Well, it's nice to know my chase is Edwards' finest."

"Nothing but the best for you nice contractors."

Schalk got down to business. He outlined his mission—a Mach 2 run in the F-104A—and briefly sketched the flight plan.

"Suppose we do this," Kinch suggested, looking at his

watch. "We'll both roll at nine forty-five. I'll take off to the south and you take off to the north from Palmdale. We'll both turn to the west and I'll pick you up in the burner climb."

Schalk agreed.

"Now, if you miss me after take-off, I'll be in a climbing right turn and—"

"Don't worry, dad," Kinch said. "I'll be there."

"O. K.," said Schalk, "I know you will. Just don't do the maneuver with me. It would degrade my bonus payments."

They checked their watches and were on their way.

At nine forty, Kinch started up the engine of his F-104 and started to taxi. Five minutes later he was at the take-off end of the 22 runway, which headed south and slightly west. He called the tower.

"Edwards, seven seventy-two, Number One on runway twenty-two."

"Roger, you are cleared for take-off."

Kinch eased the throttle forward and the sleek interceptor started to roll, slowly at first, then faster as the powerful jet sucked in increasing quantities of air. He lifted the plane easily, made a slight turn toward Palmdale and started the climb.

He was just below two thousand feet when it happened, the sudden emergency which makes life or death a matter of split-second decision—and luck. With a gasping rumble, the engine quit. Through Kinch's computer-like mind the alternatives raced swiftly. There appeared little chance of stretching the glide to a nearby dry lake; the F-104 was dropping fast. He would have to eject, but not downward; he was too low. He would have to roll her over—and did he have time?

He made the decision in a fraction of a second and started

to roll the powerless airplane, which was dropping rapidly, calling the tower simultaneously:

"Edwards, Mayday seven seventy-two, bailing out!"

The ground was rushing up crazily. He was about three-quarters of the way through the roll and he realized he couldn't complete it. He pulled the ejector. The canopy flew off, there was a sharp report, and Kinch was out of the airplane, but very low.

The F-104 smashed into the ground with a terrific impact, the fuel ignited and burst into a billowing cloud of black smoke. Kinch, his 'chute streaming, not fully opened, followed the plane, right into the deadly cloud.

In the calm wind, the telltale cloud rose straight up for a thousand feet, bringing Schalk in the air and the watchers in the tower its tragic message. Iven Kincheloe was dead.

The funeral service was held at Arlington National Cemetery, in whose beautiful grounds lie so many of the nation's heroes. The chapel was filled to capacity. In the front, with his parents, sat Dorothy Kincheloe, carrying inside her the baby her husband was never to see. Behind them were row upon row of Kinch's friends, for practically everyone who ever met him was a friend. They came from all over the country, and from abroad; there were school friends, friends from his early flying days, Korean flyers, test pilots, and top officers of the Air Force.

They heard the chaplain sum up the life of one of the great men of his time:

"We come to honor and pay tribute to one who has made a profound and indelible contribution to our national defense and the United States Air Force. Captain Iven C. Kincheloe's flying genius and achievements have come about because of his intense love of flying and constant loyalty to the Air Force.

Iven possessed a skill, courage, and devotion to his military tasks which cause us to pay him the highest respects afforded military leaders of all time. To his monumental life of activity nothing can be added in words because he is enshrined in the hearts of the youth of our nation and we are all a grateful people of these United States of America."